Fabric *Play*
Change the Fabric, Change the Quilt

Deanne Moore

Martingale®
Create with Confidence

Dedication

For my children, Tommy, Tori, Henry, and Greta, who cheered me on from start to finish, and my parents, Forrest and Shyrl, who provide unconditional strength and support through all my adventures.

Fabric Play: Change the Fabric, Change the Quilt
© 2014 by Deanne Moore

Martingale®
19021 120th Ave. NE, Ste. 102
Bothell, WA 98011-9511 USA
ShopMartingale.com

Printed in China

19 18 17 16 15 14   8 7 6 5 4 3 2 1

Library of Congress Cataloging-in-Publication Data is available upon request.

ISBN: 978-1-60468-421-6

Mission Statement

Dedicated to providing quality products and service to inspire creativity.

Credits

PUBLISHER AND CHIEF VISIONARY OFFICER: Jennifer Erbe Keltner

EDITOR IN CHIEF: Mary V. Green

DESIGN DIRECTOR: Paula Schlosser

MANAGING EDITOR: Karen Costello Soltys

ACQUISITIONS EDITOR: Karen M. Burns

TECHNICAL EDITOR: Nancy Mahoney

COPY EDITOR: Marcy Heffernan

PRODUCTION MANAGER: Regina Girard

COVER AND INTERIOR DESIGNER: Connor Chin

PHOTOGRAPHER: Brent Kane

ILLUSTRATOR: Anne Moscicki

Resources

The following companies have generously provided support and materials for the projects in this book:

- Andover Fabrics
- Benartex
- Marcus Brothers Textiles
- Maywood Studios
- Michael Miller Fabrics
- Moda
- Northcott
- Quilters Dream Batting
- The Quilt Haus
- Urban Elementz

Contents

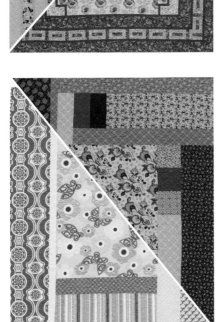

Introduction

Surrounding myself with quilters nearly every day at my quilt shop in central Texas, I've watched as the modern quilting movement has grown and become an integral part of the quilting world. I've personally found it very curious and intriguing that most quilters feel a need to take sides and declare themselves either modern or traditional.

From a strictly practical perspective, as opposed to an academic or esoteric one, Jane Quilter tends to identify a quilt as "modern" based on a small group of elements:

- Asymmetrical designs
- Large amounts of negative space
- Lack of common or traditional elements (quilt blocks, sashing, borders, etc.)
- Use of contemporary prints, solid fabrics, and nontraditional color combinations
- Simplicity of construction, often due to the sizes of the pieces

Conversely, she'll label a quilt as "traditional" if it contains most or all of these characteristics:

- Extensive piecing, usually on a small scale (1" to 4" basic units, for example)
- Rigid structure (symmetry, blocks, sashing, borders)
- Familiar color palettes and small- to medium-scale prints
- Use of traditional elements like appliqué, basic units, and common quilt blocks.
- Large investment of time, due to the difficulty level or the sheer number of pieces

"But wait!" I want to say. Traditional quilting and modern quilting don't have to be mutually exclusive! There are infinite opportunities to combine the two, and in doing so, quilting takes on a grand sense of freedom and adventure.

Most self-proclaimed traditional or modern quilters will venture cautiously into the alternate reality when pressed, and then thoroughly enjoy the adventure, and even seek out additional opportunities to explore the world new to them. While there may be differences in the aesthetics of modern and traditional quilting, there are similarities as well, and endless ways to blend the two. Quilts that successfully combine aspects of both worlds have great appeal to virtually all quilters, and this book is full of such designs. The quilts within are fun and satisfying to create, to keep, and to give away. They can transform from a more modern look to a more traditional one, or vice versa, with nothing more than a change in fabric. In fact, changing the fabric is all it takes to give each version a very distinct personality. To that end, you might notice that each quilt *pattern* is named, yet *each rendition* of the pattern also has its own unique name. Think about it . . . you wouldn't give two different children the same name, just because they're in the same family!

The best part is, all of these quilts are achievable. They can be pieced in an afternoon, or at most, a day or two. After all, the more great quilts you can make, the more great fabrics you get to play with!

A Wonderland of Fabrics

What is my favorite part of quilting? Choosing the fabrics, of course! I love the transformation that a single quilt pattern can undergo when it's made multiple times, in multiple versions. Simple changes like color placement will give a quilt pattern a fresh look, while big changes in value placement or in fabric style can actually make it look like a different pattern altogether. Take time to look through the quilt photos in this book, and then read over the list of options in the "Change the Fabric, Change the Quilt" boxes, and yes, stop and actually imagine the quilt pattern made up in the different styles listed. Be flexible too! Notice when a particular fabric is used in more than one position within a quilt, and if one fabric is replaced by two different fabrics in the alternate version or vice versa. You are allowed and even encouraged to repeat fabrics, or to ignore the indicated repeats, to achieve whatever look is most pleasing to you. Begin training yourself to imagine every quilt you see made up with a different look. Before long, you'll want to start seeing some of those visions become reality.

The sheer number of quality, 100% cotton fabrics available to today's quilters is quite simply astonishing. Visit any two quilt shops and you're likely

Attractive and acceptable (yet predictable) fabric combinations

The same combinations of fabric, with a little spark added. Notice how the cheddar solid is bright but also lighter in value than most of the prints.

to find that the number of fabrics that they *do not* have in common is far greater than the number of fabrics that they do. With the vast number of choices available, don't deny yourself the opportunity to make the most of them!

If you need a good excuse to step out of your box, choose an achievable quilt pattern and a special person to make it for—someone with very different tastes from yours. Then go on the hunt for the fabrics he or she would most like, even if they're ones that you normally don't choose. If the pattern you're making is relatively quick, you'll get it done, and likely enjoy the process. Conversely, if you choose a pattern that takes hours, days, or weeks of cutting and piecing, and you're having to spend all that time in such close proximity with fabrics that you don't particularly like, or aren't very comfortable with, that project is likely to be pushed aside in favor of, say, vacuuming, and eventually end up in a box in your already overcrowded quilting closet.

If this is still too big a leap for you, it's OK to start slow. For example, if you *never* voluntarily put yellow fabric in a quilt (on my personal planet, it's pink), then consciously decide to incorporate some yellow as a minor player in your next quick project. If you have trouble choosing a suitable yellow, don't be afraid to ask for opinions. The staff at your local quilt shop is very accustomed to helping with fabric selection and offering opinions, and your quilting friends won't be shy about speaking up either. Inevitably, at least one person you encounter is bound to think that a spark of yellow is just the thing for your project, and will help you find a yellow fabric to use. The new color may grow on you as you sew it into your quilt!

Yes, every now and again, you may actually *not like* the result of this adventure into new territory. Remember, though, it's just fabric, and there's plenty more. You can always donate your quilt top to a charity quilting group; I promise it will be deeply appreciated even with the yellow. But don't be afraid to try again. The more often you step outside your box, the more comfortable you become doing so. Eventually, that box will just melt away, and the newfound freedom to make quilts in previously unimagined colors, styles, and fabric combinations will be both refreshing and invigorating! I'll enable you, too. Design sheets following each project give you the freedom to play with fabrics, colors, and value placement. It's like being in kindergarten again: you can just have fun, and your grade is based only on completion!

"Shiloh After All: Autumn Gathering," 44½" x 54½",
designed by Deanne Moore; pieced by Diane Tarpey; quilted by Guy and Kathy Ackerson.

This quilt, simply a collection of squares and rectangles, uses the fabrics to make a statement. Combine a great feature print, a number of related fabrics, and a graphic layout to create an ideal baby quilt, a wall hanging, or a small throw.

Materials

Yardage is based on 42"-wide fabric.

¼ yard *each* of 4 assorted tone on tones for sections B and C

¾ yard of tan floral for section A

⅝ yard of brown print #3 for section D

⅓ yard of orange tone on tone for sections A and C

⅓ yard of brown print #1 for section A

⅓ yard of brown print #2 for section B

⅓ yard of tan print for section C

⅓ yard of green plaid for sections C and D

¼ yard of gold plaid for sections B and C

½ yard of brown print #4 for binding

3 yards of fabric for backing

53" x 63" piece of batting

Cutting

From the tan floral, cut:
1 rectangle, 22" x 28"

From the orange tone on tone, cut:
1 strip, 4" x 22"
1 strip, 4" x 34½"

From brown print #1, cut:
1 strip, 9" x 22"

From 2 of the assorted tone on tones, cut:
1 square, 5½" x 5½" (2 total)

From 1 of the assorted tone on tones, cut:
1 square, 5½" x 5½"
1 rectangle, 4" x 8"

From 1 of the assorted tone on tones, cut:
1 rectangle, 4" x 8"

From the gold plaid, cut:
1 strip, 5½" x 25"
1 rectangle, 4" x 11½"

From brown print #2, cut:
1 strip, 8" x 40"

From the tan print, cut:
1 strip, 8" x 24"

From the green plaid, cut:
1 strip, 4" x 31"
2 strips, 2" x 42"

From brown print #3, cut:
2 strips, 9" x 42"

From brown print #4, cut:
6 strips, 2¼" x 42"

Making the Sections

1. To make section A, join the tan-floral rectangle, orange 4" x 22" strip, and brown #1 strip as shown. Press the seam allowances toward the orange strip.

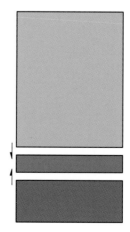

Section A

2. To make section B, join the tone-on-tone 5½" squares and gold-plaid 25"-long strip. Press the seam allowances in one direction. Sew the brown #2 strip to the pieced strip as shown. Press the seam allowances toward the brown strip.

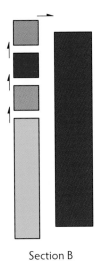

Section B

3. To make section C, join the tone-on-tone 4" x 8" rectangles and the tan 8" x 24" strip to make a pieced strip. Press the seam allowances in one direction. Sew the green-plaid 4" x 31" strip to the pieced strip, as shown in the diagram following step 4. Press the seam allowances toward the green strip.

4. Sew the gold-plaid rectangle to the left side of the unit from step 3. Press the seam allowances toward the just-added rectangle. Then sew the orange 4" x 34½" strip to the top of the unit to complete section C. Press the seam allowances toward the orange strip.

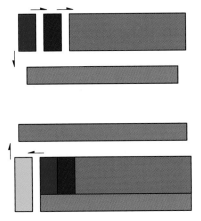

Section C

5. For section D, sew the brown #3 strips together end to end. Trim the pieced strip to measure 54½" long. Join the green-plaid 2"-wide strips end to end and then trim the pieced strip to 54½" long. Sew the brown #3 strip to the long edge of the green-plaid strip to make section D. Press the seam allowances toward the green strip.

Section D

Assembling the Quilt Top

1. Sew section B to the right edge of section A. Press the seam allowances toward A.

2. Sew section C to the top of the A/B section. Press the seam allowances toward C.

3. Sew section D to the left side of the A/B/C section to complete the quilt top. Press the seam allowances toward D.

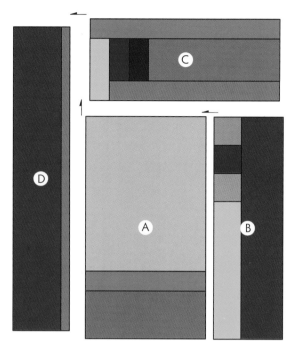

Quilt assembly

Finishing

Choose a quilting design that enhances the look and style of your quilt. Layer the quilt top, backing, and batting for quilting, or deliver them to your professional long-arm machine quilter. Referring to "Binding" on page 78, use the brown #4 strips to make and attach the binding. Attach a quilt label to the back.

Change the Fabric ○ Change the Quilt

Imagine this quilt made with . . .
- Minkee textures
- Batiks
- Country prints
- Asian prints

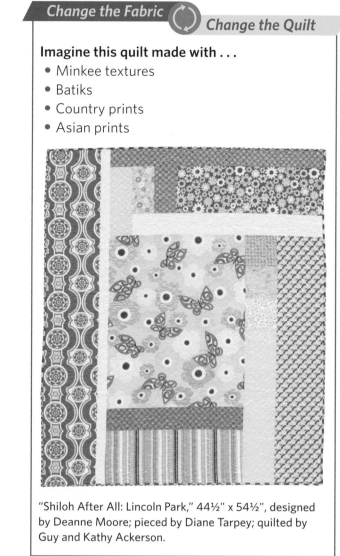

"Shiloh After All: Lincoln Park," 44½" x 54½", designed by Deanne Moore; pieced by Diane Tarpey; quilted by Guy and Kathy Ackerson.

It's Your Turn to Play!

Now it's your turn to play with fabrics and colors to make this project uniquely your own. You may want to make several photocopies of this design sheet. Use the sheets to experiment with different color combinations *before* you head to the quilt shop. Then you can make more copies when you're ready to plan your own second version of this quilt!

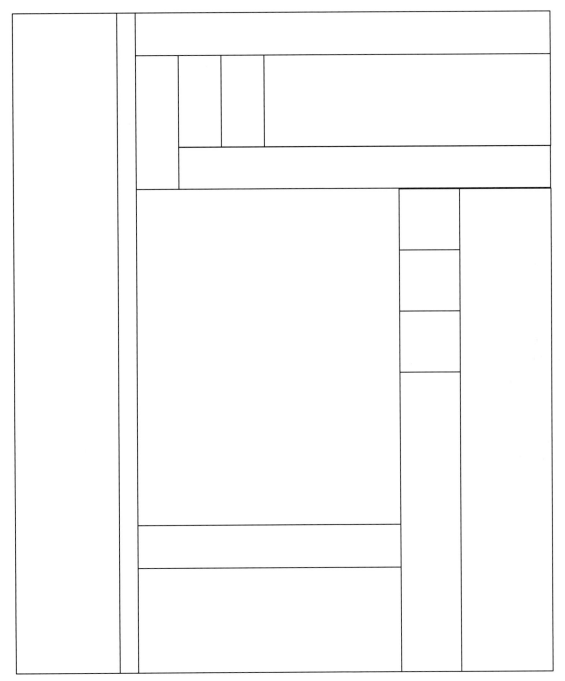

Design sheet

Changing Lanes

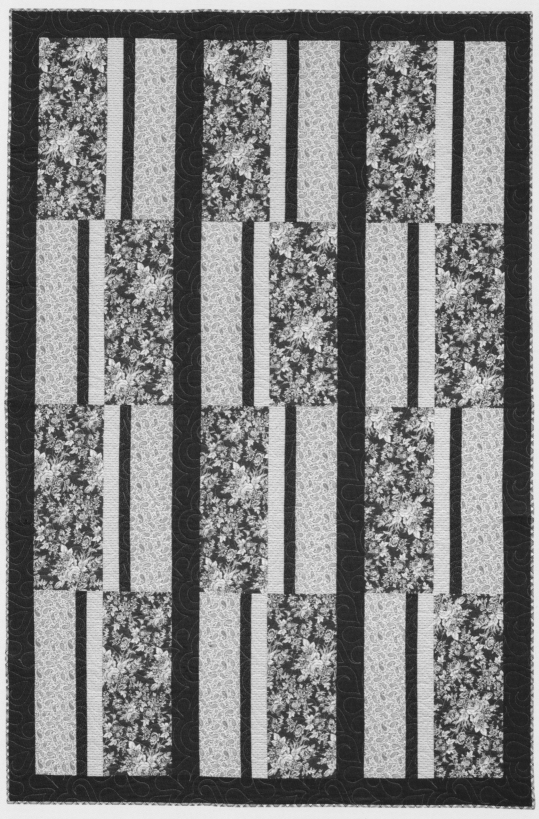

"Changing Lanes: Miss Scarlett," 57½" x 84½",
designed by Deanne Moore; pieced by Mary Jane Heinen; quilted by Laurie Shook.

*F*ast as an expressway, this quilt pattern is perfect for a quick gift. Sized as a generous throw, it will also fit nicely on a twin-size bunk bed. Easy to personalize for different tastes, it's an ideal gift for a young adult ready to experience dorm life.

Materials

Yardage is based on 42"-wide fabric.

1½ yards of red print #1 for blocks

1¼ yards of red solid for sashing and border

1 yard of red print #4 for blocks

½ yard of red print #2 for blocks

⅜ yard of red print #3 for blocks

⅝ yard of red-and-white plaid for binding

3¾ yards of fabric for backing

66" x 93" piece of batting

Cutting

From red print #1, cut:
6 strips, 8" x 42"

From red print #2, cut:
6 strips, 2¼" x 42"

From red print #3, cut:
6 strips, 1¾" x 42"

From red print #4, cut:
6 strips, 5" x 42"

From the red solid, cut:
11 strips, 3½" x 42"

From the red-and-white plaid, cut:
8 strips, 2¼" x 42"

Making the Blocks

Join red #1, #2, #3, and #4 strips, in order, along their long edges to make a strip set. Press the seam allowances in one direction. Make six strip sets. Cut each strip set into two 20"-wide segments.

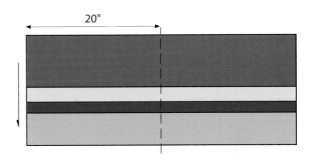

20"

Make 6 strip sets.
Cut 12 segments.

Assembling the Quilt Top

1. Sew four 20" strip-set segments together, rotating every other one, to make a column as shown in the quilt assembly diagram on page 14. Press the seam allowances in one direction. The column should measure 15½" x 78½". Make a total of three columns.

2. Join two red-solid strips end to end to make a long sashing strip. Make four long strips. Trim each strip to measure 78½" long.

3. Sew the red sashing strips and three columns together as shown in the quilt assembly diagram. Press the seam allowances toward the sashing strips.

4. Join the three remaining red-solid strips end to end. Referring to "Borders" on page 78, trim and sew the strips to the top and bottom of the quilt top to complete the border. Press the seam allowances toward the border.

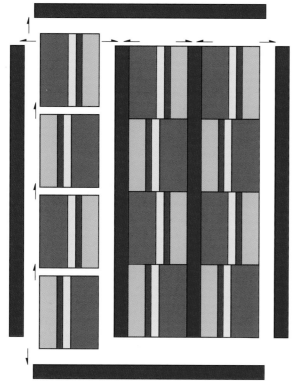

Quilt assembly

Finishing

Choose a quilting design that enhances the look and style of your quilt. Layer the quilt top, backing, and batting for quilting, or deliver them to your professional long-arm machine quilter. Referring to "Binding" on page 78, use the red-and-white plaid strips to make and attach the binding. Attach a quilt label to the back.

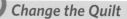

Change the Fabric ◯ *Change the Quilt*

Imagine this quilt made with . . .
- Batiks
- Children's prints
- Contemporary prints
- Patriotic fabrics

"Changing Lanes: Skyline Drive in the Fog," 57½" x 84½", designed by Deanne Moore; pieced by Maggi Oswald; quilted by Laurie Shook.

It's Your Turn to Play!

Now it's your turn to play with fabrics and colors to make this project uniquely your own. You may want to make several photocopies of this design sheet. Use the sheets to experiment with different color combinations *before* you head to the quilt shop. Then you can make more copies when you're ready to plan your own second version of this quilt!

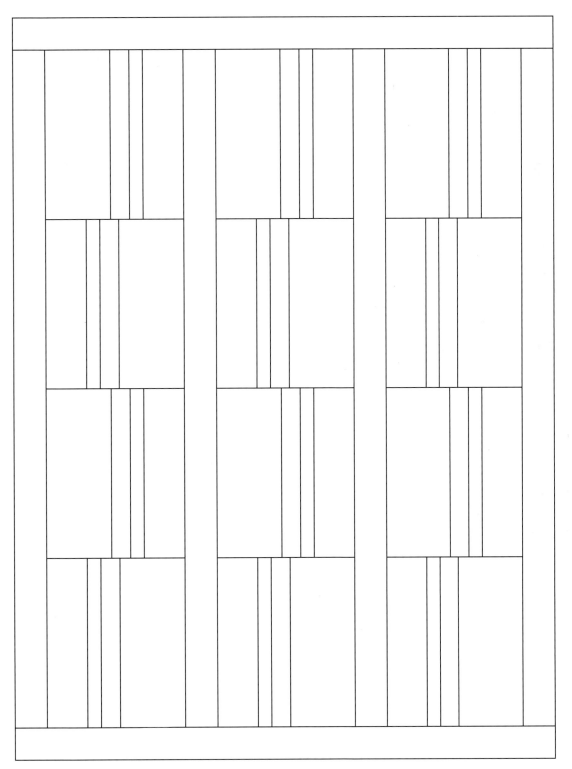

Design sheet

Garden Fence

"Garden Fence: Butterfly Garden," 93½" x 107",
designed by Deanne Moore; pieced by Nita Leinneweber; quilted by Guy and Kathy Ackerson.

The large focal center of this quilt with its attractively shaped frame, the detailed corners, and the pieced outer border combine to make this queen- or king-size quilt a beautiful addition to any bedroom. The style of the fabrics transports it from old-fashioned to elegant, from romantic to contemporary.

Materials

Yardage is based on 42"-wide fabric.

3⅝ yards of gold tone on tone for inner border, pieced border, and outer border

2½ yards of green tone on tone for accent strips, borders, and binding

1¾ yards of cream butterfly print for sections C, D, and E

1⅓ yards of medium-scale purple floral for pieced border

1⅛ yards of beige floral for sections A and B

1⅛ yards of small-scale purple floral for sections B, C, D, and E

8½ yards of fabric for backing

102" x 115" piece of batting

Cutting

From the beige floral, cut:
　1 rectangle, 23½" x 32"
　2 rectangles, 9½" x 14"
　4 squares, 5" x 5"

From the green tone on tone, cut:
　11 strips, 2¼" x 42"
　38 strips, 1½" x 42"; crosscut *14 of the strips* into:
　　2 strips, 1½" x 34½"
　　2 rectangles, 1½" x 23½"
　　2 rectangles, 1½" x 23"
　　2 rectangles, 1½" x 14"
　　12 rectangles, 1½" x 6"
　　4 rectangles, 1½" x 5½"
　　20 rectangles, 1½" x 5"
　　12 rectangles, 1½" x 4½"

From the small-scale purple floral, cut:
　5 strips, 5" x 42"; crosscut into:
　　2 strips, 5" x 34½"
　　2 rectangles, 5" x 23"
　　4 rectangles, 5" x 8½"
　　4 squares, 5" x 5"
　2 strips, 4½" x 42"; crosscut into:
　　4 rectangles, 4½" x 8½"
　　4 squares, 4½" x 4½"

From the cream butterfly print, cut:
　4 strips, 9½" x 42"; crosscut into:
　　2 strips, 9½" x 41"
　　4 rectangles, 9½" x 13"
　2 strips, 7½" x 36½"
　4 squares, 5" x 5"
　4 squares, 4½" x 4½"

From the medium-scale purple floral, cut:
　20 strips, 2" x 42"

From the gold tone on tone, cut:
　10 strips, 5½" x 42"
　8 strips, 5¼" x 42"
　10 strips, 2" x 42"

> **TIP**
>
> ### Fitting Notes
>
> An accurate ¼" seam allowance is very important in this project so the pieces will fit together exactly. Correct orientation of the pieces is critical as well, so pay close attention to the reversed sections. Refer to the illustrations in each section for placement guidance throughout. After sewing each seam, press the seam allowances in the direction indicated.

Making the Center Sections

Section A

Sew a green 1½" x 23½" rectangle to each short side of the beige-floral 23½" x 32" rectangle to make section A. The section should measure 23½" x 34".

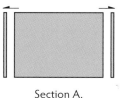

Section A.
Make 1.

Section B

Refer to the illustration following step 6 throughout.

1. Sew a green 1½" x 14" rectangle to one long side of a beige-floral 9½" x 14" rectangle. Repeat to make a second unit.

2. Sew green 1½" x 5" rectangles to the short ends of a small-scale purple-floral 5" x 8½" rectangle. Make a total of four units.

3. Join a green 1½" x 5" rectangle to each beige-floral 5" square and each small-scale purple-floral 5" square. Make four of each unit.

4. Sew a green 1½" x 6" rectangle between a purple unit with the green strip at the bottom and a beige unit with the green strip at the top. Then sew a unit from step 2 to the top of the unit. Repeat to make a second unit.

5. Reversing the positions of the beige unit and the purple unit, make two reversed units.

6. Sew one unit from step 4 and one unit from step 5 to one unit from step 1, carefully orienting the units as shown, to make one B section. The section should measure 10½" x 34". Repeat to make a second B section.

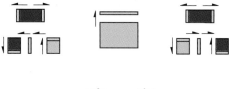

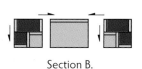

Section B.
Make 2.

Section C

1. Sew a green 1½" x 23" rectangle to one long side of a small-scale purple-floral 5" x 23" rectangle. Then sew a green 1½" x 6" rectangle to each end of the unit. Repeat to make a second unit.

2. Sew a green 1½" x 5" rectangle to each cream-butterfly 5" square. Make a total of four units.

3. Sew a cream unit to each end of a unit from step 1 as shown to make one C section. The section should measure 6" x 34". Repeat to make a second C section.

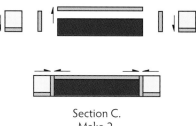

Section C.
Make 2.

Section D

1. Sew a green 1½" x 34½" strip to one long side of a small-scale purple-floral 5" x 34½" strip. Sew green 1½" x 6" rectangles to the short ends of the unit. Repeat to make a second unit.

2. Sew a cream-butterfly 7½" x 36½" strip to the green strip on one unit from step 1.

3. Sew cream-butterfly 9½" x 13" rectangles to the top and bottom of the unit from step 2 to make one D section. The section should measure 13" x 54½".

4. Repeat steps 2 and 3 to make a second D section.

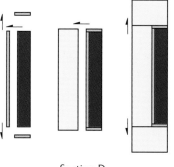

Section D.
Make 2.

Section E

Refer to the illustration following step 4 throughout.

1. Sew a green 1½" x 4½" rectangle to one end of each small-scale purple-floral 4½" x 8½" rectangle. Make a total of four units.

2. Join a green 1½" x 4½" rectangle to each cream-butterfly 4½" square and to each small-scale purple-floral 4½" square. Make four of each unit.

3. Sew a green 1½" x 5½" rectangle between a purple unit with the green strip at the bottom and a cream unit with the green strip at the top. Sew a unit from step 1 to the top of the unit. Repeat to make a second unit. Reversing the positions of the cream unit and the purple unit, make two reversed units.

4. Sew a regular and a reversed unit from step 3 to the ends of a cream-butterfly 9½" x 41" strip, carefully orienting the units as shown to make one E section. The section should measure 9½" x 59". Repeat to make a second E section.

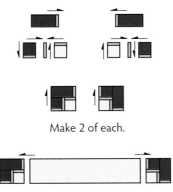

Make 2 of each.

Section E.
Make 2.

Making the Pieced Border

1. Referring to "Strip Sets" on page 77, sew medium-scale purple-floral strips to both long edges of a gold 2"-wide strip to make a strip set. Make 10 strip sets. From the strip sets, cut 74 segments, 5" wide.

5"

Make 10 strip sets.
Cut 74 segments.

2. Sew 19 segments together, rotating every other segment, to make one side border strip. Press the seam allowances in the directions indicated. The border strip should measure 5" x 86". Starting with the opposite orientation, make a second border strip.

3. Sew 18 segments together, rotating every other segment, to make the top border. Press the seam allowances in the directions indicated. The border strip should measure 5" x 81½". Repeat to make an identical strip for the bottom border.

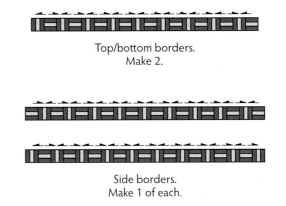

Top/bottom borders.
Make 2.

Side borders.
Make 1 of each.

Assembling the Quilt Top

After sewing each seam, press the seam allowances in the directions indicated.

1. Join the A and B sections. Sew the C sections to the top and bottom of the center section.

2. Sew the D sections to opposite sides of the center section. Then sew the E sections to the top and bottom edges to complete the quilt-top center. The quilt-top center should measure 59" x 72½".

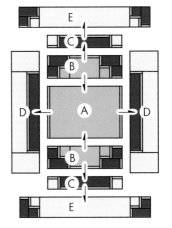

Quilt assembly

3. Join seven of the green 1½"-wide strips end to end. Refer to "Borders" on page 78 to measure the length of the quilt top. From the pieced strip, cut two strips to this length and sew them to the sides of the quilt top. Measure the width of the quilt top. From the remainder of the pieced strip, cut two strips to this length and sew them to the top and bottom of the quilt top. The quilt top should measure 61" x 74½".

4. In the same manner, sew the gold 5¼"-wide strips end to end; measure, cut, and sew them to the quilt top. The quilt top should measure 70½" x 84".

5. In the same manner, sew eight of the green 1½"-wide strips end to end; measure, cut, and sew them to the quilt top. The quilt top should measure 72½" x 86".

6. Sew the 19-segment pieced border strips to the sides of the quilt top. Sew the 18-segment pieced border strips to the top and bottom of the quilt top, orienting the borders so the pattern of alternating blocks is continuous.

7. Repeat step 3, sewing the remaining green 1½"-wide strips end to end; measure, cut, and sew them to the quilt top.

8. Sew the gold 5½"-wide strips end to end; measure, cut, and sew them to the quilt top to complete the outer border.

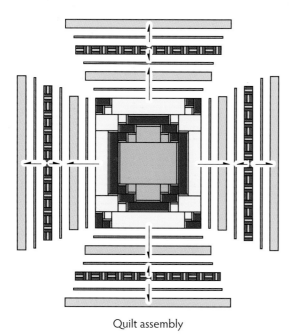

Quilt assembly

TIP

Adjusting Pieced-Border Lengths

If your quilt does not measure 72½" x 86", you'll need to adjust the length of the pieced borders. To make the border a little longer, make several seam allowances a little bit smaller. To make the border a little shorter, make several of the seam allowances a little bit bigger. Space out the seams you're redoing along the entire length of the border.

Finishing

Choose a quilting design that enhances the look and style of your quilt. Layer the quilt top, backing, and batting for quilting, or deliver them to your professional long-arm machine quilter. Referring to "Binding" on page 78, use the green 2¼"-wide strips to make and attach the binding. Attach a quilt label to the back.

Change the Fabric **Change the Quilt**

Imagine this quilt made with . . .
- Christmas prints
- Civil War reproduction prints
- Elegant Jacobean prints
- Modern minimal prints

"Garden Fence: Greta's Garden," 93½" x 107", designed by Deanne Moore; pieced by Maggi Oswald; quilted by Guy and Kathy Ackerson.

It's Your Turn to Play!

Now it's your turn to play with fabrics and colors to make this project uniquely your own. You may want to make several photocopies of this design sheet. Use the sheets to experiment with different color combinations *before* you head to the quilt shop. Then you can make more copies when you're ready to plan your own second version of this quilt!

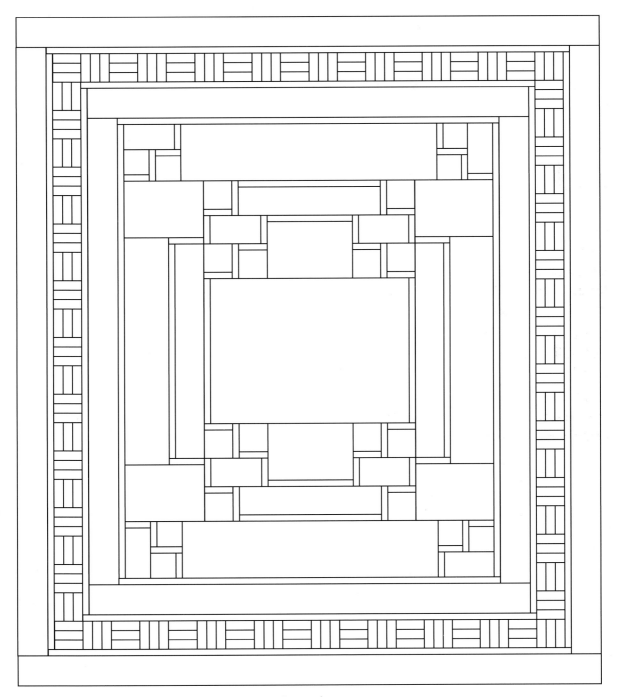

Design sheet

Manhattan

"Manhattan: Portugal," 60½" x 75½",
designed by Deanne Moore; pieced by Maggi Oswald; quilted by Kelleigh Sommer.

This throw-sized quilt may be modern in style, but the pattern is versatile enough to showcase a coordinated collection of nine fabrics in absolutely any theme!

Materials

Yardage is based on 42"-wide fabric. Fat quarters are approximately 18" x 21".

1 fat quarter *each* of 9 assorted feature prints for blocks

⅝ yard *each* of 9 assorted solids for blocks

⅝ yard of multicolored print for binding

4 yards of fabric for backing

69" x 84" piece of batting

Cutting

From *each* assorted print, cut:*
  1 rectangle, 8½" x 13½" (9 total)
  2 strips, 1½" x 16½" (18 total)
  2 strips, 1½" x 19½" (18 total)

From *each* assorted solid, cut:
  2 strips, 3½" x 42"; crosscut into:
    2 rectangles, 3½" x 13½" (18 total)
    2 rectangles, 3½" x 14½" (18 total)
  2 strips, 2½" x 20½" (18 total)
  2 strips, 2½" x 21½" (18 total)

From the multicolored print, cut:
  8 strips, 2¼" x 42"

*For directional prints, cut the large rectangles parallel to the selvage as shown below. In this case, you'll need to cut additional 1½"-wide strips. Join each 1½" x 6" strip to a 1½" x 16" strip. Trim each pieced strip to make two 1½" x 19½" strips.

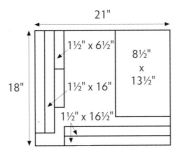

Cutting diagram for directional print running parallel to selvage.

Making the Blocks

Before you begin sewing, pair the rectangles and strips from one assorted solid with the rectangles from one assorted print. After sewing each seam, press the seam allowances in the directions indicated by the arrows.

1. Sew solid 3½" x 13½" rectangles to opposite sides of a print 8½" x 13½" rectangle. Sew solid 3½" x 14½" rectangles to the top and bottom of the print rectangle.

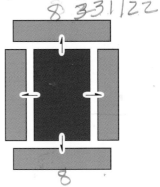

2. Sew print 1½" x 19½" strips to opposite sides of the unit from step 1. Sew print 1½" x 16½" strips to the top and bottom of the unit.

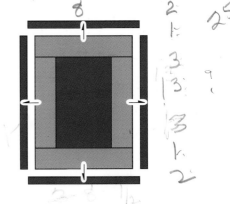

3. Sew solid 2½" x 21½" strips to opposite sides of the unit from step 2. Sew solid 2½" x 20½" strips to the top and bottom of the unit to

make one block. Repeat the steps to make a total of nine blocks.

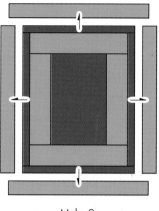

Make 9.

Assembling the Quilt Top

Arrange the blocks in three rows of three blocks each. When you are pleased with the arrangement, sew the blocks into rows. Press the seam allowances in opposite directions from row to row. Sew the rows together to complete the quilt top; press the seam allowances in one direction.

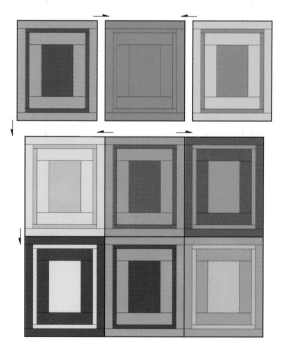

Quilt assembly

Finishing

Choose a quilting design that enhances the look and style of your quilt. Layer the quilt top, backing, and batting for quilting, or deliver them to your professional long-arm machine quilter. Referring to "Binding" on page 78, use the multicolored strips to make and attach the binding. Attach a quilt label to the back.

Change the Fabric Change the Quilt

Imagine this quilt made with . . .
- Amish solids
- Sports prints
- Autumn fabrics
- Pretty florals
- Even T-shirts!

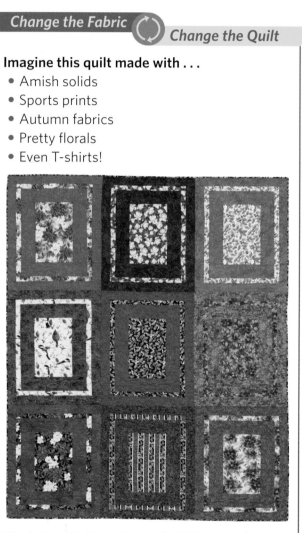

"Manhattan: Christmas Frames," 60½" x 75½", designed by Deanne Moore; pieced and quilted by Dea Heller.

It's Your Turn to Play!

Now it's your turn to play with fabrics and colors to make this project uniquely your own. You may want to make several photocopies of this design sheet. Use the sheets to experiment with different color combinations *before* you head to the quilt shop. Then you can make more copies when you're ready to plan your own second version of this quilt!

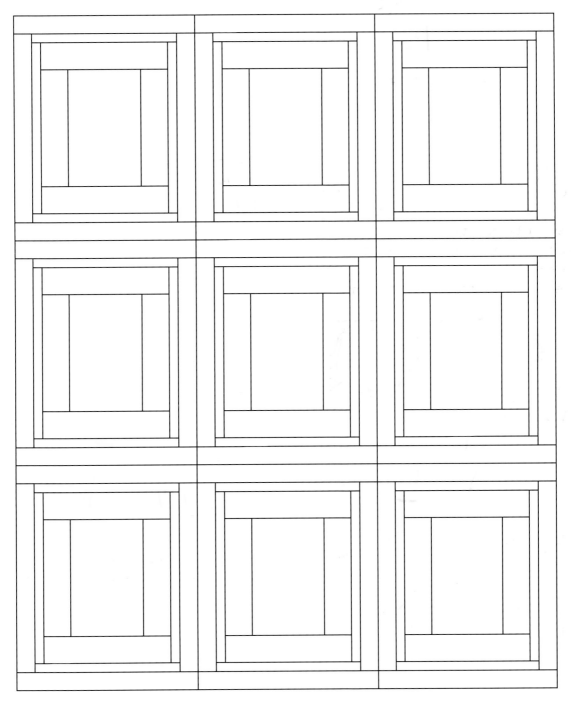

Design sheet

Mercury Falling

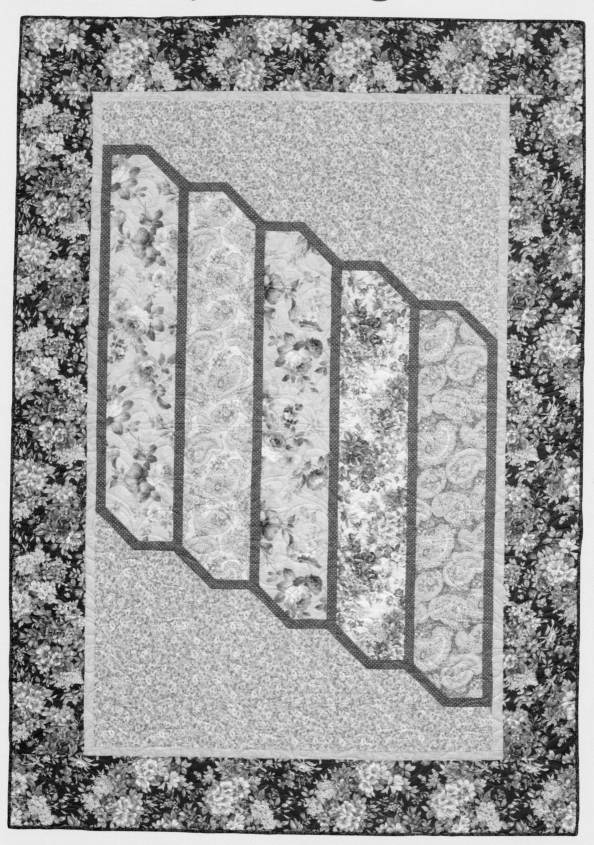

"Mercury Falling: Della Mae," 62½" x 88½",
designed and quilted by Deanne Moore; pieced by Mary Jane Heinen.

A gentle cascade of framed focal prints draws attention to this quilt, regardless of the style of fabrics used. The large borders make the quilt perfect for featuring atop a twin-size bed.

Materials

Yardage is based on 42"-wide fabric.

2 yards of dark-blue floral for outer border

⅓ yard *each* of 5 assorted blue-and-yellow prints for blocks

1⅛ yards of light-blue floral for background

⅝ yard of medium-blue dot for blocks

⅜ yard of yellow tone on tone for inner border

⅝ yard of blue tone on tone for binding

4 yards of fabric for backing

71" x 97" piece of batting

Cutting

From *each* of the assorted blue-and-yellow prints, cut:
   1 strip, 7½" x 40½" (5 total)

From the light-blue floral, cut:
   1 strip, 8½" x 42"; crosscut into:
      1 rectangle, 5" x 8½"
      1 rectangle, 8½" x 21"
      1 strip, 1½" x 8½"
      5 squares, 3½" x 3½"
   1 strip, 9½" x 42"; crosscut into:
      1 rectangle, 5" x 9½"
      1 rectangle, 9½" x 21"
      5 squares, 4½" x 4½"
   2 strips, 8½" x 42"; crosscut *each* strip into:
      1 rectangle, 8½" x 9" (2 total)
      1 rectangle, 8½" x 13" (2 total)
      1 rectangle, 8½" x 17" (2 total)

From the medium-blue dot, cut:
   1 strip, 4" x 42"; crosscut into 10 squares,
      4" x 4"
   5 strips, 1½" x 40½"
   3 strips, 1½" x 42"; crosscut 2 of the strips into:
      10 strips, 1½" x 8½"
      5 squares, 1½" x 1½"

From the yellow tone on tone, cut:
   6 strips, 1½" x 42"

From the *lengthwise grain* of the dark-blue floral, cut:
   4 strips, 10" x 72"

From the blue tone on tone, cut:
   8 strips, 2¼" x 42"

Making the Blocks

1. Refer to "Stitch-and-Flip Corners" on page 77. Sew blue-dot 4" squares to opposite corners of each blue-and-yellow rectangle as shown to make five rectangular units.

Make 5.

2. Sew a blue-dot 1½" x 40½" strip to the right side of each rectangular unit. Press the seam allowances toward the blue strip.

Make 5.

3. Sew blue-dot 1½" x 8½" rectangles to the top and bottom of each unit to make five sections. Press the seam allowances toward the blue rectangles.

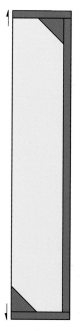

Make 5.

4. Sew a light-blue 4½" square to the *upper-right* corner of each section. Sew a light-blue 3½" square to the *lower-left* corner of each section. Make five blocks.

Make 5.

Making the Setting Blocks

Referring to the photo on page 26 and the quilt assembly diagram on page 30, arrange the floral blocks on a design wall or other flat surface.

1. Using the "Stitch-and-Flip Corners" method and orienting the pieces as shown, sew blue-dot 1½" squares to the upper-right corners of a light-blue 9½" x 21" rectangle, 8½" x 17" rectangle, 8½" x 13" rectangle, and 8½" x 9" rectangle to make four setting blocks.

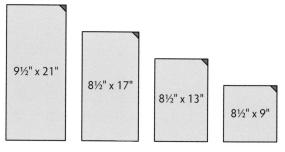

9½" x 21" 8½" x 17" 8½" x 13" 8½" x 9"

Make 1 of each.

2. Sew a blue-dot 1½" square to the upper-right corner of the light-blue 1½" x 8½" strip. Sew this unit to one end of the blue-dot 1½" x 42" strip. Then sew the pieced strip to the far-left block, matching the seam intersections as shown. Trim the ends of the strip even with the edges of the block.

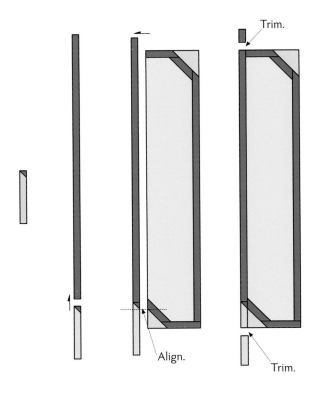

Assembling the Quilt-Top Center

1. Lay out the blocks, setting blocks, and light-blue rectangles as shown. Join the pieces to make five columns. Press the seam allowances in the directions indicated by the arrows.

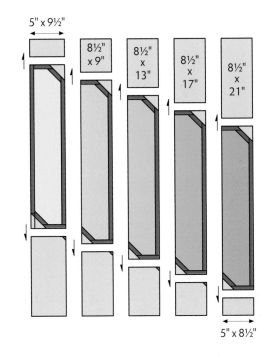

2. Sew the five columns together, carefully matching the seam intersections as shown.

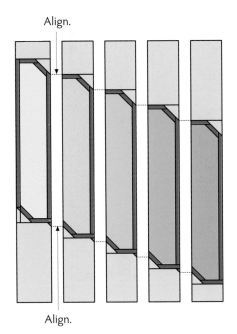

3. Join the yellow 1½"-wide strips end to end. Refer to "Borders" on page 78 to measure the length of the quilt top. From the pieced strip, cut two strips to this length and sew them to the sides of the quilt top. Press the seam allowances toward the border strips. Measure the width of the quilt top. From the remainder of the pieced strip, cut two strips to this length and sew them to the top and bottom of the quilt top to complete the inner border. Press the seam allowances toward the inner border.

4. In the same way, measure, cut, and sew the dark-blue floral strips to the quilt top for the outer border. Press all seam allowances toward the outer border.

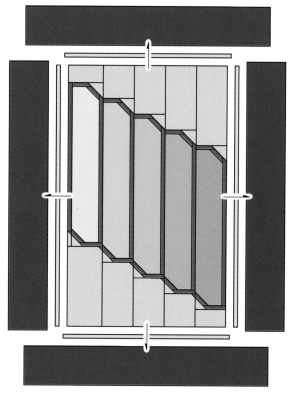

Quilt assembly

Finishing

Choose a quilting design that enhances the look and style of your quilt. Layer the quilt top, backing, and batting for quilting, or deliver them to your professional long-arm machine quilter. Referring to "Binding" on page 78, use the blue tone-on-tone strips to make and attach the binding. Attach a quilt label to the back.

Change the Fabric | **Change the Quilt**

Imagine this quilt made with . . .
- Ombrés
- Children's prints
- Western-themed prints
- Asian prints
- Taupe prints

"Mercury Falling: On the Boardwalk," 62½" x 88½", designed and quilted by Deanne Moore; pieced by Mary Jane Heinen.

It's Your Turn to Play!

Now it's your turn to play with fabrics and colors to make this project uniquely your own. You may want to make several photocopies of this design sheet. Use the sheets to experiment with different color combinations *before* you head to the quilt shop. Then you can make more copies when you're ready to plan your own second version of this quilt!

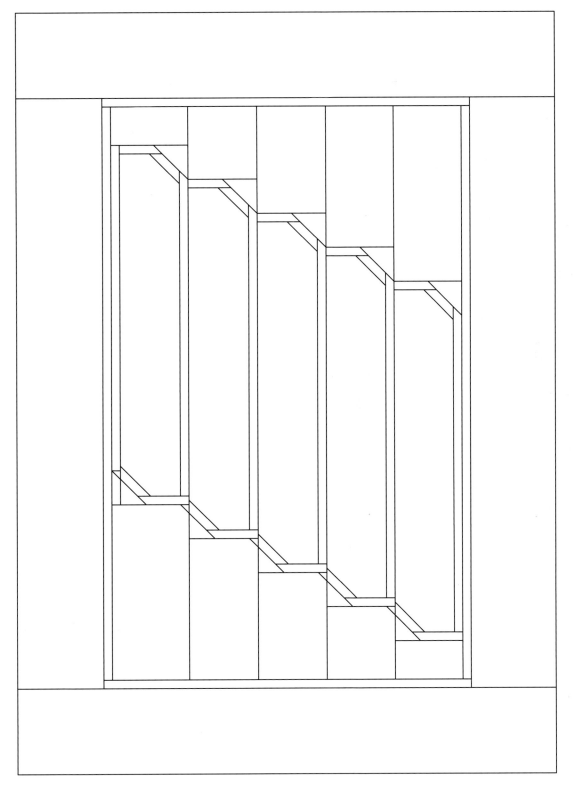

Design sheet

"Messages: Tori at 2," 61" x 83",
designed by Deanne Moore; pieced by Terry Hughes; quilted by Patricia Ritter.

T*he arrangement of print rectangles in this simple quilt reminds me of a stream of text messages on my cell phone screen! This quilt is graphic and eye-catching on a twin bed or perfect as a large throw. (It also makes a special gift for a tall man, if made in a different color scheme.)*

Materials

Yardage is based on 42"-wide fabric. Fat quarters are approximately 18" x 21".

1 fat quarter *each* of 8 assorted pink, yellow, and orange prints for blocks

2½ yards of white dot for background

1 yard of pink solid for accent strips

⅝ yard of orange solid for binding

4 yards of fabric for backing

70" x 92" piece of batting

Cutting

From *each* of the fat quarters, cut:
 3 rectangles, 6" x 17" (24 total; 1 will be extra)

From the white dot, cut:
 2 strips, 22½" x 42"; crosscut into 28 strips, 2¾" x 22½"
 1 strip, 28" x 42"; crosscut into 14 strips, 2¾" x 28"
 2 strips, 2¾" x 42"; crosscut into 2 strips, 2¾" x 28"

From the pink solid, cut:
 1 strip, 28" x 42"; crosscut into:
 8 strips, 1½" x 28"
 14 strips, 1½" x 22½"

From the orange solid, cut:
 8 strips, 2¼" x 42"

Making the Strip Blocks

1. Sew a white-dot 2¾" x 28" strip to each long edge of a pink 1½" x 28" strip to make a 28"-long strip block. Press the seam allowances toward the pink strip. Make a total of eight strip blocks.

Make 8.

2. Sew a white-dot 2¾" x 22½" strip to each long edge of a pink 1½" x 22½" strip to make a 22½"-long strip block. Press the seam allowances toward the pink strip. Make a total of 14 strip blocks.

Make 14.

Assembling the Quilt Top

1. Sew a pink, yellow, or orange rectangle to each end of a 28"-long strip block to make an A row. Press the seam allowances toward the rectangles. Make eight rows.

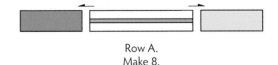

Row A.
Make 8.

2. Sew a 22½"-long strip block to each end of a pink, yellow, or orange rectangle to make a B row. Press the seam allowances toward the rectangle. Make seven rows.

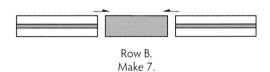

Row B.
Make 7.

3. Sew the A and B rows together, alternating them as shown in the quilt assembly diagram. Press the seam allowances in one direction.

Quilt assembly

Finishing

Choose a quilting design that enhances the look and style of your quilt. Layer the quilt top, backing, and batting for quilting, or deliver them to your professional long-arm machine quilter. Referring to "Binding" on page 78, use the orange-solid strips to make and attach the binding. Attach a quilt label to the back.

Referring to "Binding" on page 78

Change the Fabric **Change the Quilt**

Imagine this quilt made with . . .
- 1930s reproduction prints
- Seasonal prints
- Sports fabrics
- Patriotic prints

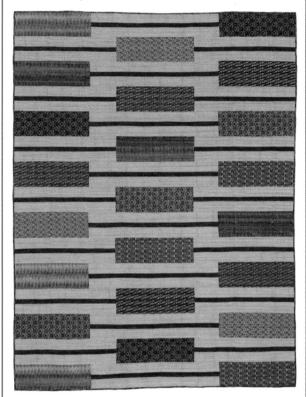

"Messages: Rustic Modern," 61" x 83", designed by Deanne Moore; pieced by Terry Hughes; quilted by Patricia Ritter.

It's Your Turn to Play!

Now it's your turn to play with fabrics and colors to make this project uniquely your own. You may want to make several photocopies of this design sheet. Use the sheets to experiment with different color combinations *before* you head to the quilt shop. Then you can make more copies when you're ready to plan your own second version of this quilt!

Design sheet

Roam

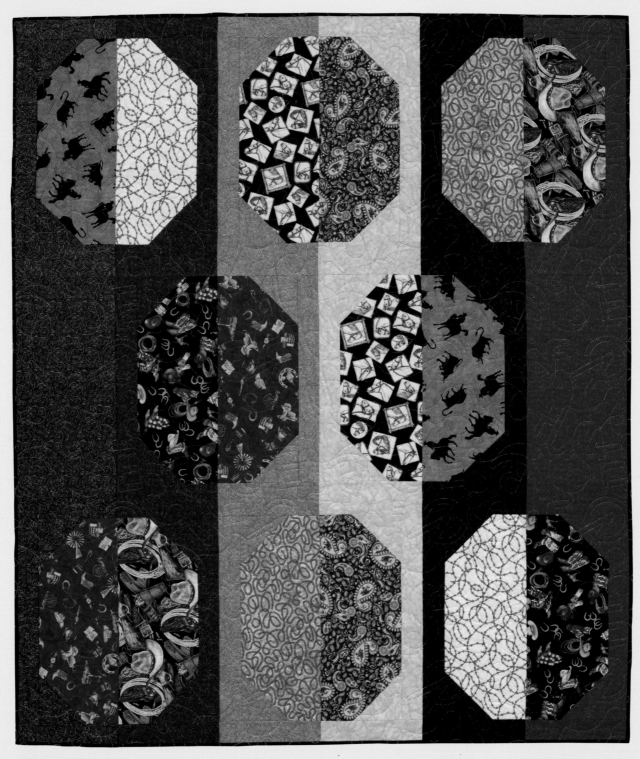

"Roam: Eight Seconds," 57½" x 67½",
designed by Deanne Moore; pieced by Mary Jane Heinen; quilted by Kelleigh Sommer.

The eight featured blocks in this fun throw quilt seem to float three-dimensionally above the striated background, resulting in a unique look that is graphically appealing.

Materials

Yardage is based on 42"-wide fabric. Fat quarters are approximately 18" x 21".

1 fat quarter *each* of 8 assorted Western prints for blocks

½ yard *each* of 4 assorted tone on tones for inner columns

⅝ yard *each* of 2 assorted tone on tones for outer columns

⅝ yard of black tone on tone for binding

3¾ yards of fabric for backing

66" x 76" piece of batting

TIP

Planning Fabric Placement

It's important to plan the placement of the different fabrics in this quilt prior to cutting and piecing the blocks. First, determine the position of the tone-on-tone fabrics for the vertical columns. Then decide on the arrangement of the assorted Western prints. There are many symmetrical options for their placement, yet a random, scattered arrangement works just as well.

Cutting

From *each* of the assorted Western prints, cut:
2 rectangles, 8" x 19½" (16 total)

From *each* of the assorted tone on tones for outer columns, cut:
1 strip, 10" x 42"; crosscut into:
2 rectangles, 2½" x 10" (4 total)
2 rectangles, 3½" x 10" (4 total)
1 rectangle, 10" x 19½" (2 total)

1 strip, 2½" x 42"; crosscut into 2 strips, 2½" x 19½" (4 total)
4 squares, 5" x 5" (8 total)

From *each* of the assorted tone on tones for inner columns, cut:
2 rectangles, 2½" x 10" (8 total)
2 rectangles, 3½" x 10" (8 total)
3 strips, 2½" x 19½" (12 total)
6 squares, 5" x 5" (24 total)

From the black tone on tone, cut:
7 strips, 2¼" x 42"

Making the Blocks

1. Refer to "Stitch-and-Flip Corners" on page 77. Sew matching tone-on-tone 5" squares to top- and bottom-left corners of a Western-print rectangle to make a rectangular unit. Press the seam allowances toward the resulting triangles. Make a total of 16 units.

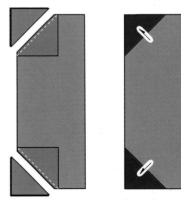

Make 16.

2. Sew a matching tone-on-tone 2½" x 19½" strip to one side of a unit from step 1 as shown to make a block. Press the seam allowances

toward the just-added rectangle. Make a total of 16 blocks.

Make 16.

Assembling the Quilt Top

1. Lay out the blocks and tone-on-tone 10" x 19½" rectangles in three rows as shown in the quilt assembly diagram below. Arrange the tone-on-tone 3½" x 10" rectangles in two rows of six rectangles each, placing them between the block rows and matching the colors to the blocks they'll touch as shown below. Then arrange the tone-on-tone 2½" x 10" rectangles in two rows of six rectangles each, placing them above the top block row and below the bottom block row, as shown below.

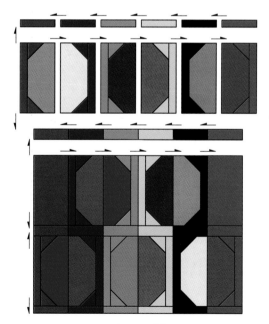

Quilt assembly

2. Join the blocks and rectangles into horizontal rows. Press the seam allowances in the directions indicated below left.

3. Join the rows and press the seam allowances in the directions indicated below left.

Finishing

Choose a quilting design that enhances the look and style of your quilt. Layer the quilt top, backing, and batting for quilting, or deliver them to your professional long-arm machine quilter. Referring to "Binding" on page 78, use the black tone-on-tone strips to make and attach the binding. Attach a quilt label to the back.

Change the Fabric ↻ *Change the Quilt*

Imagine this quilt made with . . .
- Asian prints
- Children's prints
- Seasonal prints
- Contemporary prints

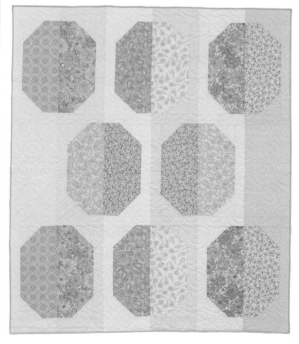

"Roam: Sorbet," 57½" x 67½", designed by Deanne Moore; pieced by Wendy Kinard; quilted by Laurie Shook.

It's Your Turn to Play!

Now it's your turn to play with fabrics and colors to make this project uniquely your own. You may want to make several photocopies of this design sheet. Use the sheets to experiment with different color combinations *before* you head to the quilt shop. Then you can make more copies when you're ready to plan your own second version of this quilt!

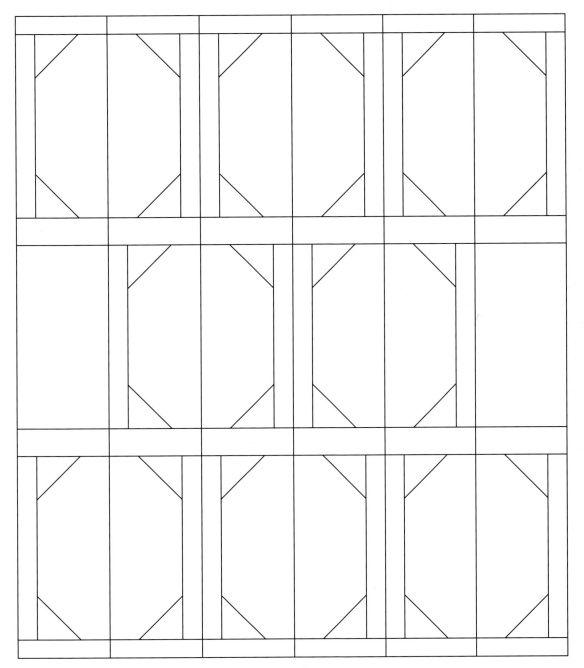

Design sheet

Sticks and Stones

"Sticks and Stones: Crayons," 44½" x 62",
designed by Deanne Moore; pieced by Mary Jane Heinen; quilted by Kelleigh Sommer.

The upper and lower pieced sections add a certain panache to the simple center of this lap-sized quilt. Seminole piecing makes the sewing quick and easy; the fabric choices make this a one-of-a-kind quilt.

Materials

Yardage is based on 42"-wide fabric.

⅜ yard *each* of red, orange, yellow, green, blue, and purple tone on tones for center strips

1⅛ yards of turquoise fabric for border

1 yard of multicolored dot for accent squares and binding

3 yards of fabric for backing

53" x 70" piece of batting

Cutting

From *each* of the red, orange, yellow, green, blue, and purple tone on tones, cut:
- 1 strip, 6" x 29" (6 total)
- 6 squares, 4⅜" x 4⅜" (36 total)

From the multicolored dot, cut:
- 28 squares, 4⅜" x 4⅜"
- 6 strips, 2¼" x 42"

From the turquoise fabric, cut:
- 2 strips, 6" x 29"
- 2 strips, 6" x 39"
- 8 squares, 4⅜" x 4⅜"; cut *4 of the squares* in half diagonally to yield 8 triangles
- 4 rectangles, 3¼" x 17"

Assembling the Quilt Top

1. Sew the 6" x 29" turquoise, red, orange, yellow, green, blue, and purple tone-on-tone strips together along their long edges in the order shown to make the center section of the quilt. Press the seam allowances in one direction.

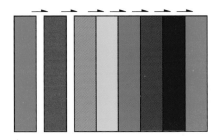

2. Join the multicolored squares and the turquoise, red, orange, yellow, green, blue, and purple tone-on-tone squares as shown to make one set of eight strips. Pay careful attention to color placement. Press the seam allowances toward the tone-on-tone squares. Repeat to make a second set of eight strips.

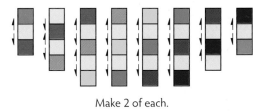

Make 2 of each.

3. Sew together one set of strips from step 2, matching the seam intersections as shown. Press the seam allowances in one direction. Make two units.

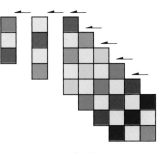

Make 2.

4. Use a ruler and rotary cutter to trim and square up each unit from step 3, making sure to leave ¼" beyond the points of all the multi-colored squares for seam allowance.

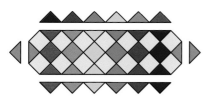

5. With right sides together, center and sew a turquoise triangle to each corner of a unit from step 4. Press the seam allowances toward the turquoise triangles. In the same way, sew turquoise triangles on the corners of the second unit.

Make 2.

6. Lay out the center section, the units from step 5, the turquoise 6" x 39" strips, and the turquoise 3¼" x 17" rectangles as shown in the quilt assembly diagram. Join the pieces to make the top and bottom sections. Press the seam allowances toward the turquoise pieces.

7. Sew the top and bottom sections to the center section, aligning the seam intersections. Press the seam allowances toward the center section.

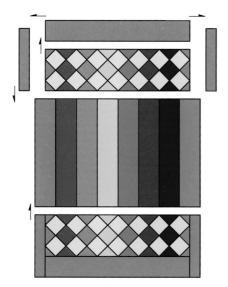

Quilt assembly

Finishing

Choose a quilting design that enhances the look and style of your quilt. Layer the quilt top, backing, and batting for quilting, or deliver them to your professional long-arm machine quilter. Referring to "Binding" on page 78, use the multicolored strips to make and attach the binding. Attach a quilt label to the back.

Change the Fabric ⟳ **Change the Quilt**

Imagine this quilt made with . . .
- Civil War reproduction prints
- Contemporary prints
- Florals
- Solids

"Sticks and Stones: Palaces of Sand," 44½" x 62", designed by Deanne Moore; pieced by Mary Jane Heinen; quilted by Kelleigh Sommer.

It's Your Turn to Play!

Now it's your turn to play with fabrics and colors to make this project uniquely your own. You may want to make several photocopies of this design sheet. Use the sheets to experiment with different color combinations *before* you head to the quilt shop. Then you can make more copies when you're ready to plan your own second version of this quilt!

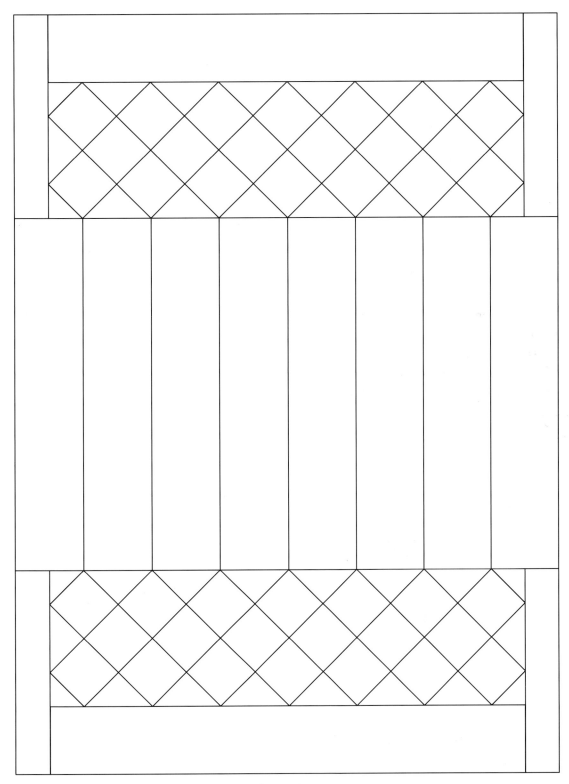

Design sheet

Structure

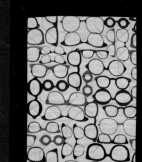

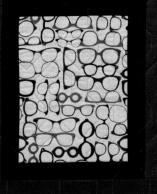

"Structure: It's a Guy Thing," 51½" x 60½",
designed by Deanne Moore; pieced by Terry Hughes; quilted by Laurie Shook.

A structured arrangement of fun, funky prints, a formal garden of planter boxes, or a classic collage of anything you choose—this throw has a clean, fresh, and boldly geometric look in any fabric style.

Materials

Yardage is based on 42"-wide fabric.

1⅓ yards of black solid for blocks and binding

1⅓ yards of gray solid for sashing and border

½ yard of gray novelty print #1 for center block*

½ yard of gray novelty print #2 for blocks

⅜ yard of gray novelty print #3 for blocks*

¼ yard of gray novelty print #4 for blocks*

3⅓ yards of fabric for backing

60" x 69" piece of batting

If you are using directional prints, you'll need 1 yard of gray print #1 and ½ yard each of gray prints #3 and #4.

Cutting

From gray #1, cut:
1 rectangle, 12½" x 27½"

From gray #3, cut:
2 rectangles, 9½" x 15½"

From gray #4, cut:
2 rectangles, 6½" x 12½"

From gray #2, cut:
4 rectangles, 9½" x 12½"

From the black solid, cut:
1 strip, 12½" x 42"; crosscut into 20 rectangles, 2" x 12½"
7 strips, 2" x 42"; crosscut into:
 2 rectangles, 2" x 27½"
 4 rectangles, 2" x 6½"
 10 rectangles, 2" x 15½"
6 strips, 2¼" x 42"

From the gray solid, cut:
12 strips, 3½" x 42"; crosscut *3 of the strips* into:
 4 rectangles, 3½" x 12½"
 2 rectangles, 3½" x 15½"

Making the Blocks

1. To make block A, sew black 2" x 27½" rectangles to opposite long sides of the gray #1 rectangle. Sew black 2" x 15½" rectangles to the top and bottom of the rectangle to complete the block. Press all seam allowances toward the black rectangles.

2. To make block B, sew black 2" x 15½" rectangles to opposite long sides of the gray #3 rectangle. Sew black 2" x 12½" rectangles to the top and bottom of the rectangle to complete the block. Press all seam allowances toward the black rectangles. Make two blocks.

3. To make block C, sew black 2" x 6½" rectangles to opposite short sides of the gray #4 rectangle. Sew black 2" x 15½" rectangles to the top and bottom of the rectangle to complete the block. Press all seam allowances toward the black rectangles. Make two blocks.

4. To make block D, sew black 2" x 12½" rectangles to opposite long sides of the gray #2 rectangle. Sew black 2" x 12½" rectangles to the top and bottom of the rectangle to complete the block. Press all seam allowances toward the black rectangles. Make four blocks.

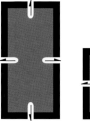
Block A.
Make 1.

Block B.
Make 2.

Block C.
Make 2.

Block D.
Make 4.

Assembling the Quilt Top

Refer to the photo on page 44 and the quilt assembly diagram below for placement guidance throughout.

1. Sew together one B block, two D blocks, and two gray-solid 3½" x 12½" rectangles as shown to make an outer column. Press the seam allowances toward the gray rectangles. Repeat to make a second outer column.

2. Sew together the A block, C blocks, and gray-solid 3½" x 15½" rectangles as shown to make the center column. Press the seam allowances toward the gray rectangles.

3. Join the gray-solid 3½"-wide strips end to end. Refer to "Borders" on page 78 to measure the length of the columns; they should measure 54½" long. From the pieced strip, cut four 54½"-long strips. Sew the three columns and four gray strips together, alternating them as shown. Press the seam allowances toward the gray strips.

4. Measure the width of the quilt top. From the remaining gray pieced strip, cut two strips to this length and sew them to the top and bottom of the quilt top. Press the seam allowances toward the gray strips.

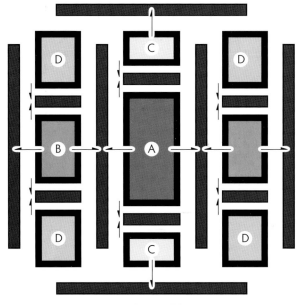

Quilt assembly

Finishing

Choose a quilting design that enhances the look and style of your quilt. Layer the quilt top, backing, and batting for quilting, or deliver them to your professional long-arm machine quilter. Referring to "Binding" on page 78, use the black 2¼"-wide strips to make and attach the binding. Attach a quilt label to the back.

Change the Fabric ○ **Change the Quilt**

Imagine this quilt made with . . .
- Western-themed prints
- Civil War reproduction prints
- Americana fabrics
- Theme fabrics (sport, hobby, etc.)

"Structure: Juliette," 51½" x 60½", designed and quilted by Deanne Moore; pieced by Terry Hughes.

It's Your Turn to Play!

Now it's your turn to play with fabrics and colors to make this project uniquely your own. You may want to make several photocopies of this design sheet. Use the sheets to experiment with different color combinations *before* you head to the quilt shop. Then you can make more copies when you're ready to plan your own second version of this quilt!

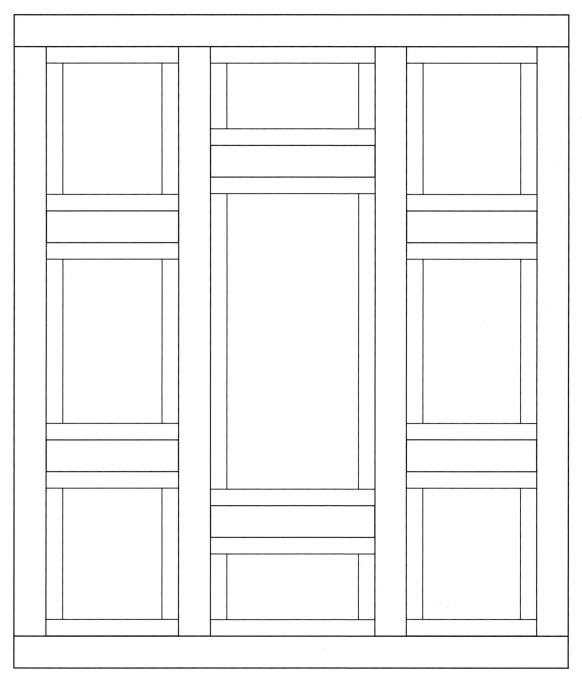

Design sheet

Go Your Own Way

"Go Your Own Way: Slow Down You Crazy Child," 54½" x 71½",
designed by Deanne Moore; pieced by Shirley Ginn; quilted by Laurie Shook.

*W*ith striking angled strips of flying geese framing a feature print, and wide strips completing the graphic design, this quilt is eye-catching in any style of fabric.

Materials

Yardage is based on 42"-wide fabric.

¼ yard *each* of red, dark-blue, chartreuse, deep-pink, medium-blue, orange, teal, lime-green, and medium-pink tone on tone for sections A, B, C, and D

1¼ yards of blue-and-green floral for flying-geese units and binding

1⅛ yards of red dot for outer border

¾ yard of dark-fuchsia tone on tone for flying-geese units

⅝ yard of multicolored print for center rectangle

⅜ yard of green stripe for inner border

3½ yards of fabric for backing

63" x 80" piece of batting

Square ruler, 15" x 15" or larger

Cutting

From the multicolored print, cut:
1 rectangle, 18½" x 30½"

From the blue-and-green floral, cut:
3 strips, 7¼" x 42"; crosscut into 11 squares, 7¼" x 7¼". Cut 1 of the squares into quarters diagonally to yield 4 triangles (2 will be extra).
7 strips, 2¼" x 42"

From the dark-fuchsia tone on tone, cut:
4 strips, 3⅞" x 42"; crosscut into 40 squares, 3⅞" x 3⅞"
2 squares, 7¼" x 7¼"; cut 1 of the squares into quarters diagonally to yield 4 small triangles (2 will be extra). Cut the remaining square in half diagonally to yield 2 large triangles.

From the chartreuse tone on tone, cut:
1 rectangle, 6½" x 8"
1 rectangle, 6½" x 22"
1 rectangle, 6½" x 10"

From the deep-pink tone on tone, cut:
1 rectangle, 6½" x 14"
1 rectangle, 6½" x 24"

From the medium-blue tone on tone, cut:
2 rectangles, 6½" x 20"

From the orange tone on tone, cut:
1 rectangle, 6½" x 24"
1 rectangle, 6½" x 14"

From the teal tone on tone, cut:
1 rectangle, 6½" x 22"
1 rectangle, 6½" x 8"
1 rectangle, 6½" x 10"

From the red tone on tone, cut:
1 rectangle, 6½" x 22"*

From the dark-blue tone on tone, cut:
1 rectangle, 6½" x 34"*

From the lime-green tone on tone, cut:
1 rectangle, 6½" x 34"*

From the medium-pink tone on tone, cut:
1 rectangle, 6½" x 22"*

From the green stripe, cut:
6 strips, 1½" x 42"

From the red dot, cut:
6 strips, 5" x 42"

*The lengths of these pieces are intentionally over-sized to allow for trimming.

Making the Sections

1. Refer to "Flying-Geese Units, Method A" on page 76. Use four dark-fuchsia 3⅞" squares and one blue-and-green square to make one set of four flying-geese units. Make a total of 10 sets of four flying-geese units (40 units).

Make 40.

2. Join 10 flying-geese units to make a strip. Press the seam allowances in one direction. Make a total of four strips.

3. Sew one flying-geese strip to each long side of the multicolored rectangle, rotating one strip as shown, to make the center section. Press the seam allowances toward the center.

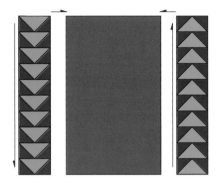

4. Join the chartreuse 6½" x 8" rectangle, the deep-pink 6½" x 14" rectangle, one medium-blue rectangle, the orange 6½" x 24" rectangle, and the teal 6½" x 22" rectangle, aligning the right edges as shown, to make section A. Press the seam allowances in one direction.

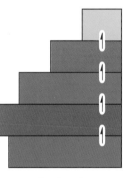

Section A

5. Join the chartreuse 6½" x 22" rectangle, the deep-pink 6½" x 24" rectangle, one medium-blue rectangle, the orange 6½" x 14" rectangle, and the teal 6½" x 8" rectangle, aligning

the left edges as shown, to make section B. Press the seam allowances in one direction.

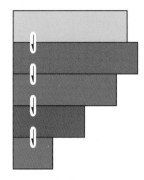

Section B

6. Sew a blue-and-green triangle to a dark-fuchsia triangle of the same size. Press the seam allowances toward the dark-fuchsia triangle. Make two units.

7. Sew a triangle unit from step 6 to one end of a flying-geese strip. Sew a large dark-fuchsia triangle to the other end of the same strip as shown. Press the seam allowances toward the dark-fuchsia triangles. Repeat to make a second strip.

8. Fold the teal 6½" x 10" rectangle, the red rectangle, and the dark-blue rectangle in half and finger-press to mark the center. Aligning the center creases, sew the three rectangles together and press the seam allowances in one direction.

9. Center and sew the strip unit from step 8 to one strip from step 7 as shown to make section C.

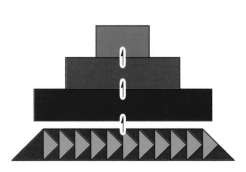

Section C

10. In the same way, join the lime-green rectangle, the medium-pink rectangle, and the chartreuse 6½" x 10" rectangle. Center and sew the strip unit to the remaining strip from step 7 to make section D.

11. Sew section A to the left side of the center section, matching the seam intersections. Press the seam allowances toward section A. Sew section B to the right side of the center section in the same manner and press.

12. Sew section C to the top of the section from step 11, matching the seam intersections. Sew section D to the bottom of the section to complete the quilt-top center. Press all seam allowances toward the center section.

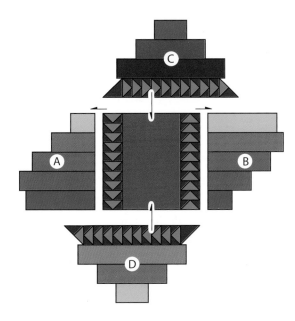

Trimming the Quilt-Top Center

1. Lay a large square ruler on a long side of the quilt top along the flying-geese strip, with the 45° line on one of the seam lines. Measuring ¼" from the points of the flying geese, carefully mark a line. Move the ruler along the side of the quilt, realigning the 45° line with another seam, and continue marking the line. Repeat in the opposite direction, until one side of the quilt is marked for trimming. *Don't trim yet!* In the same manner, mark the other long side of the quilt top.

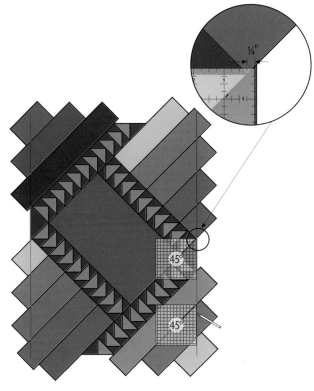

Mark sides.

2. On one short side of the quilt top, align the edge of the ruler with the edge of the triangle unit, placing the 45° line on the ruler on one of the seam lines. Mark a line across the strips. Move the ruler, realign the 45° line, and continue marking until the entire side is marked. *Again, don't trim yet!* In the same way, mark the other short side of the quilt top.

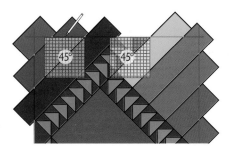

Mark top and bottom.

3. Place a large square ruler in each corner, making sure the 45° line on the ruler is parallel to a nearby seam. The marked lines should be at a 90° angle to each other. If not, re-mark the lines as needed. Take your time, making sure the lines are marked correctly, but *don't trim yet!*

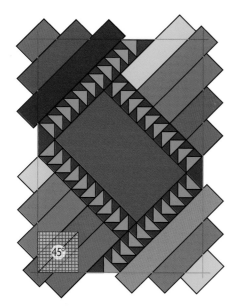

Repeat the process to sew the remaining green strip on the opposite side of the quilt-top center.

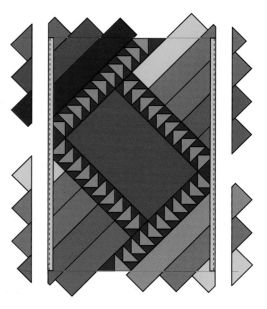

5. Measure the width of the quilt center. From the pieced green strip, cut two strips to this length. In the same manner as before, sew strips to the top and bottom of the quilt top to complete the inner border. Trim the edges of the quilt top. Press all seam allowances toward the inner border.

6. Join the red dot strips end to end referring to "Borders." Measure the length of the quilt top. From the pieced strip, cut two strips to this length and sew them to the sides of the quilt top. Measure the width of the quilt top. From the remainder of the pieced strip, cut two strips to this length and sew them to the

> ### TIP
> ### Add Borders Before Trimming
> Trimming off the excess strip edges will leave bias edges, which are prone to stretching, around the entire quilt-top center. Sewing the inner border to the center before trimming the strips will help to keep the quilt square and flat.

4. Join the green-striped strips end to end. Refer to "Borders" on page 78 to measure the length of the quilt top. From the pieced strip, cut two strips to this length. Lay a green-striped strip on one long side of the quilt-top center, right sides together. Align the edge of the strip with the marked line. Pin and sew the strip in place. Carefully trim away the edges of the quilt top. Press the seam allowances toward the border.

top and bottom of the quilt top. Press all seam allowances toward the outer border.

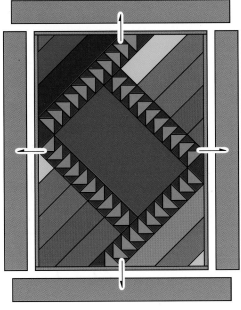

Quilt assembly

Finishing

Choose a quilting design that enhances the look and style of your quilt. Layer the quilt top, backing, and batting for quilting, or deliver them to your professional long-arm machine quilter. Referring to "Binding" on page 78, use the blue-and-green strips to make and attach the binding. Attach a quilt label to the back.

Change the Fabric **Change the Quilt**

Imagine this quilt made with . . .

- Batiks
- Taupe prints
- Holiday fabrics
- Children's prints

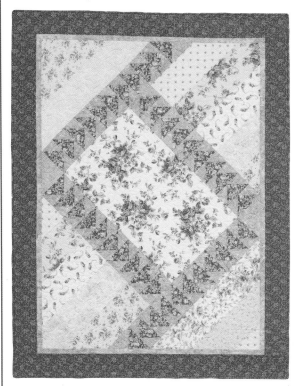

"Go Your Own Way: Sweet Briar Rose," 54½" x 71½", designed by Deanne Moore; pieced by Wendy Kinard; quilted by Laurie Shook.

It's Your Turn to Play!

Now it's your turn to play with fabrics and colors to make this project uniquely your own. You may want to make several photocopies of this design sheet. Use the sheets to experiment with different color combinations *before* you head to the quilt shop. Then you can make more copies when you're ready to plan your own second version of this quilt!

Design sheet

"Grand Windmill: Margaret," 90½" x 99½",
designed by Deanne Moore; pieced by Nita Leinneweber; quilted by Guy and Kathy Ackerson.

6 x 20 + 79 (handwritten)

-size bed quilt features a big, graphic design ideal for showcasing a favorite large-scale, nondirectional print. Make it soft and soothing, young and fun, or . . . ? It looks great in any style.

Materials

Yardage is based on 42"-wide fabric.   *10x10* (handwritten)

3⅜ yards of gray geometric print for center square and outer border   *Dk Pink* (handwritten)

2¼ yards of gray floral for center sections and middle border   *Floral   OK* (handwritten)

1¾ yards of cream floral for center sections   *yellow   OK* (handwritten)   *Need* (handwritten)

1⅛ yards of charcoal print for center sections and inner border   *Blue* (handwritten)

1 yard of taupe print for center sections   *green* (handwritten)

¼ yard of gray tone on tone for center sections   *dark pink* (handwritten)   *Need* (handwritten)

¾ yard of black tone on tone for binding

8¼ yards of fabric for backing   *Need* (handwritten)

99" x 108" piece of batting

Cutting

For the most efficient use of each fabric, cut the pieces in the order listed.

From the cream floral, cut:
   yellow (handwritten)
- 1 rectangle, 18" x 32"
- 2 strips, 13½" x 42"; crosscut into: *Cut Done* (handwritten)
  - 1 rectangle, 13½" x 27"
  - 1 rectangle, 13½" x 19"
  - 2 rectangles, 8½" x 13½"
- 1 rectangle, 10" x 21½"
- 4 squares, 7" x 7"

From the gray floral, cut: *#1* (handwritten)
   main floral (handwritten)
- 2 rectangles, 11½" x 21½"
- 1 rectangle, 11½" x 40"
- 1 rectangle, 11½" x 31"
- 8 strips, 3½" x 42"

From the taupe print, cut: *#2* (handwritten)
   Green (handwritten)   *tone* (handwritten)
- 2 rectangles, 7" x 21½"
- 1 rectangle, 7" x 40"
- 1 rectangle, 7" x 31"

From the charcoal print, cut:
- 1 strip, 13½" x 42"; crosscut into 4 rectangles, 7" x 13½"
- 8 strips, 2½" x 42"   *Dark Pink* (handwritten)

From the gray tone on tone, cut:
- 4 squares, 7" x 7"   *Blue   Done* (handwritten)   *Blue* (handwritten)

From the *lengthwise grain* of the gray geometric print, cut: *Lt Pink* (handwritten)
- 4 strips, 10" x 108"   *Border* (handwritten)
- 1 square, 10" x 10"

From the black tone on tone, cut:
- 10 strips, 2¼" x 42"

Making the Sections

Refer to the photo on page 55 and the illustrations in each section for placement guidance throughout. After sewing each seam, press the seam allowances in the direction indicated.

1. Lay out the squares and rectangles as shown. Join the gray tone-on-tone and cream-floral 7" squares. Add the charcoal 7" x 13½" rectangle, cream 8½" x 13½" rectangle, taupe 7" x 21½" rectangle, and gray-floral 11½" x 21½" rectangle to complete section A.

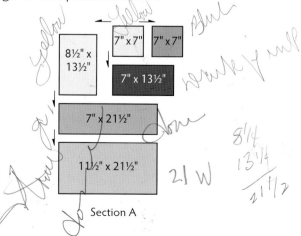

Section A

2. Lay out the squares and rectangles as shown. Join the gray tone-on-tone and cream-floral 7" squares. Add the charcoal 7" x 13½" rectangle, cream-floral 13½" x 27" rectangle, taupe 7" x 40" rectangle, and gray-floral 11½" x 40" rectangle to complete section B.

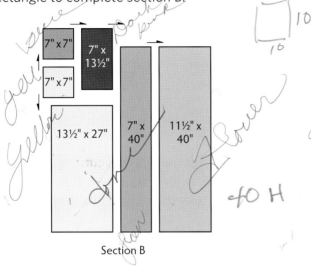

Section B

3. Lay out the squares and rectangles as shown. Join the gray tone-on-tone and cream-floral 7" squares. Add the charcoal 7" x 13½" rectangle, cream-floral 13½" x 19" and 18" x 32" rectangles, taupe 7" x 31" rectangle, and gray-floral 11½" x 31" rectangle to complete section C.

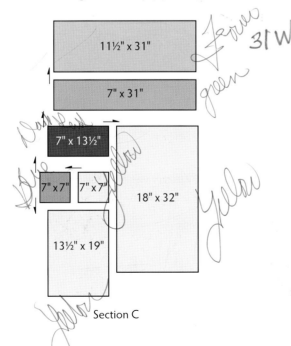

Section C

4. Lay out the squares and rectangles as shown above right. Join the gray tone-on-tone and cream-floral 7" squares. Add the charcoal

7" x 13½" rectangle, cream-floral 8½" x 13½" and 10" x 21½" rectangles, taupe 7" x 21½" rectangle, and gray-floral 11½" x 21½" rectangle to complete section D.

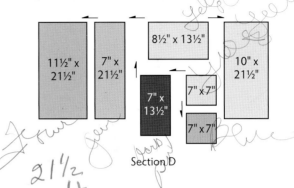

Section D

Assembling the Quilt Top

1. Arrange the four sections and the gray geometric-print square as shown below. Sew section A to the center square, stopping about 2" from the edge with a backstitch. Press the seam allowances toward the center square.

2. Sew section B to the unit from step 1; then add section C. Press the seam allowances in the directions indicated.

3. Sew the bottom edge of section D to the unit from step 2; press.

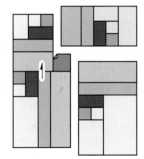
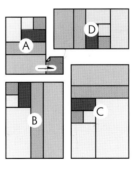
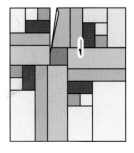
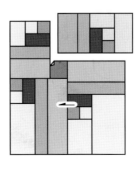

4. Sew the open part of section A and center-square seam to section D to complete the

quilt-top center. Press the seam allowances toward section D.

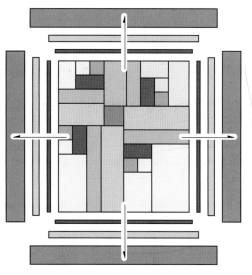

5. Join the charcoal strips end to end. Refer to "Borders" on page 78 to measure the length of the quilt top. From the pieced strip, cut two strips to this length and sew them to the sides of the quilt top. Press the seam allowances toward the border. Measure the width of the quilt top. From the remainder of the pieced strip, cut two strips to this length and sew them to the top and bottom of the quilt top to complete the inner border. Press the seam allowances toward the inner border.

6. Join the gray-floral strips end to end. In the same way, measure, cut, and sew the strips to the quilt top for the middle border. Press all seam allowances toward the middle border.

7. Join the gray geometric-print strips end to end. Measure, cut, and sew the strips to the quilt top for the outer border. Press all seam allowances toward the outer border.

Quilt assembly

Finishing

Choose a quilting design that enhances the look and style of your quilt. Layer the quilt top, backing, and batting for quilting, or deliver them to your professional long-arm machine quilter. Referring to "Binding" on page 78, use the black tone-on-tone strips to make and attach the binding. Attach a quilt label to the back.

Change the Fabric ⟳ Change the Quilt

Imagine this quilt made with . . .
- Woodsy flannels
- Batiks
- Children's prints
- Patriotic fabrics

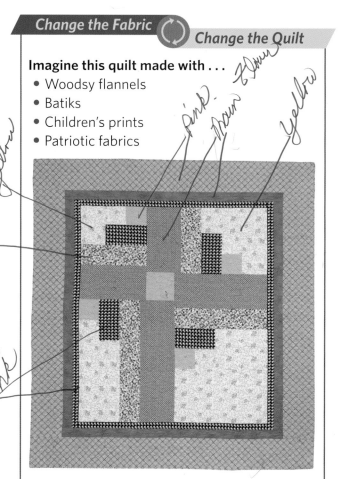

"Grand Windmill: On My Own," 90½" x 99½", designed by Deanne Moore; pieced by Shirley Ginn; quilted by Guy and Kathy Ackerson.

It's Your Turn to Play!

Now it's your turn to play with fabrics and colors to make this project uniquely your own. You may want to make several photocopies of this design sheet. Use the sheets to experiment with different color combinations *before* you head to the quilt shop. Then you can make more copies when you're ready to plan your own second version of this quilt!

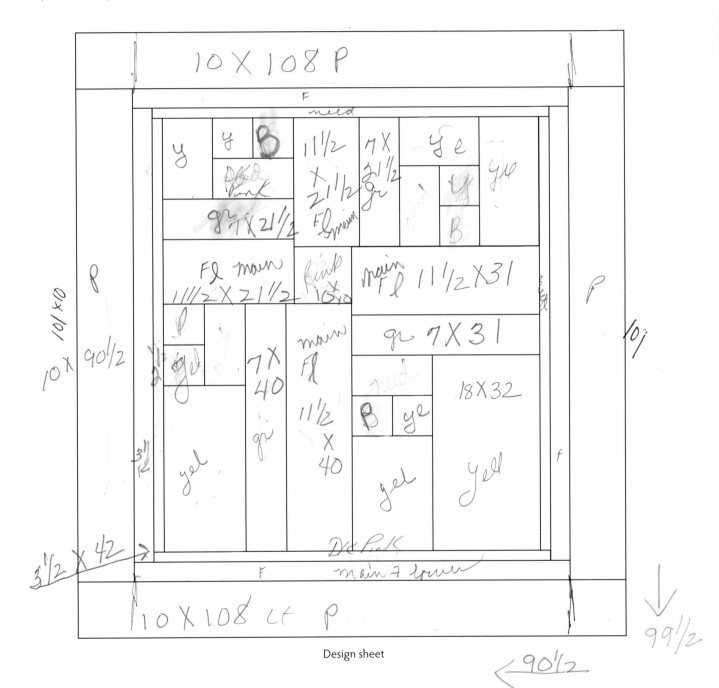

Design sheet

Hexagon Alley

"Hexagon Alley: Caterpillar," 64" x 83",
designed and quilted by Deanne Moore; pieced by Nita Leinneweber.

*S*taggering the focal columns of the quilt center, and then adding an asymmetrical background without borders, gives this graphic twin-size quilt a modern flair. With a simple change in fabric style and the addition of an outer border, it becomes a pleasing full- or queen-size quilt that will enhance any bedroom.

Materials

Yardage is based on 42"-wide fabric. Fat quarters are approximately 18" x 21".

2⅞ yards of gray batik for background

1¼ yards of turquoise batik for zigzag accent

1 fat quarter *each* of 4 assorted purple batiks for blocks

1 fat quarter *each* of 4 assorted turquoise batiks for blocks

1 yard of dark-purple batik for zigzag accent

⅝ yard of gray tone on tone for binding*

2⅝ yards of fabric for outer border (optional)

4⅛ yards of fabric for backing*

73" x 92" piece of batting*

*If you add an outer border, you'll need ¾ yard of fabric for binding, 7¾ yards for backing, and a 92" x 111" piece of batting.

Cutting

From *each* of the fat quarters, cut:
   1 rectangle, 11½" x 18½" (8 total)

From the dark-purple batik, cut:
   3 strips, 6" x 42"; crosscut into:
      16 squares, 6" x 6"
      1 rectangle, 6" x 11½"
   2 squares, 12¼" x 12¼"

From the turquoise batik, cut:
   3 strips, 6" x 42"; crosscut into 17 squares, 6" x 6"
   1 square, 12¼" x 12¼"
   1 strip, 6⅜" x 42"; crosscut into 5 squares, 6⅜" x 6⅜"

From the *lengthwise grain* of the gray batik, cut:
   2 strips, 6" x 44½"
   1 strip, 11½" x 64"
   1 strip, 22½" x 64"
   2 rectangles, 6" x 29½"
   9 squares, 6⅜" x 6⅜"
   1 square, 6" x 6"

From the *lengthwise grain* of the (optional) outer-border fabric, cut:
   4 strips, 10½" x 90"

From the gray tone on tone, cut:
   8 strips, 2¼" x 42"*

*If you're adding an outer border, cut 10 strips.

Making the Units

1. Referring to "Stitch-and-Flip Corners" on page 77, sew a dark-purple 6" square on each corner of a turquoise 11½" x 18½" rectangle. Make one unit from each turquoise rectangle (four total).

2. Sew a turquoise 6" square on each corner of a purple 11½" x 18½" rectangle. Make one unit from each purple rectangle (four total).

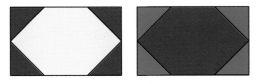

Make 4 of each.

3. Refer to "Flying-Geese Units, Method A" on page 76. Use four gray 6⅜" squares and one dark-purple 12¼" square to make four flying-geese units as shown below.

4. Use four gray 6⅜" squares and the turquoise 12¼" square to make four flying-geese units as shown below.

5. Use four turquoise 6⅜" squares and one dark-purple 12¼" square to make four flying-geese units as shown below. You'll have one extra unit.

6. Refer to "Flying-Geese Units, Method B" on page 77. Use the dark-purple 6" x 11½" rectangle, one turquoise 6" square, and the gray 6" square to make one flying-geese unit, making sure to position the turquoise square on the right end of the rectangle and the gray square on the left end as shown.

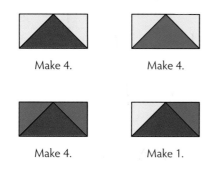

Make 4.   Make 4.

Make 4.   Make 1.

7. Refer to "Half-Square-Triangle Units" on page 76. Use one turquoise 6⅜" square and one gray 6⅜" square to make two half-square-triangle units. You'll have one extra unit.

Assembling the Quilt Top

1. Sew a purple/gray flying-geese unit to the left side of each turquoise unit. Press the seam allowances in one direction. Make a total of four units. Join the four units into a column

and press. Sew a turquoise/gray flying-geese unit to the right side of each purple unit. Press the seam allowances in one direction. Join the four units into a column; press.

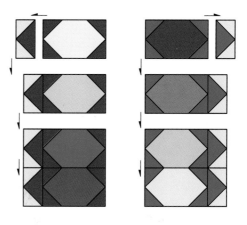

2. Sew a gray 6" x 44½" strip to the flying-geese side of each column. Press the seam allowances toward the gray strips. Sew a gray 6" x 29½" rectangle to the bottom of the turquoise column and to the top of the purple column. Press the seam allowances toward the gray rectangles.

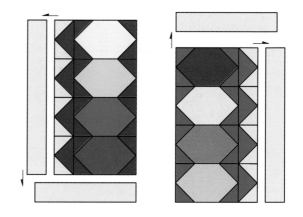

3. Lay out three purple/turquoise flying-geese units, the purple/turquoise/gray flying-geese unit, and the turquoise/gray half-square-triangle unit as shown. Join the units to make

a strip. Press the seam allowances in one direction.

4. Sew the columns from step 2 to opposite sides of the strip from step 3 as shown below. Press the seam allowances toward the center. The center section should measure 50" x 64".

5. Sew the gray 11½" x 64" strip to the top and the gray 22½" x 64" strip to the bottom of the center section. Press all seam allowances toward the gray strips.

Quilt assembly

6. Optional: Referring to "Borders" on page 78, use the 10½"-wide strips to add an outer border to the quilt top.

Finishing

Choose a quilting design that enhances the look and style of your quilt. Layer the quilt top, backing, and batting for quilting, or deliver them to your professional long-arm machine quilter. Referring to "Binding" on page 78, use the gray tone-on-tone strips to make and attach the binding. Attach a quilt label to the back.

Change the Fabric → Change the Quilt

Imagine this quilt made with . . .
- Contemporary prints
- Asian fabrics
- Flannels
- Novelty prints

"Hexagon Alley: America," 84" x 103", designed by Deanne Moore; pieced by Nita Leinneweber; quilted by Kelleigh Sommer.

It's Your Turn to Play!

Now it's your turn to play with fabrics and colors to make this project uniquely your own. You may want to make several photocopies of this design sheet. Use the sheets to experiment with different color combinations *before* you head to the quilt shop. Then you can make more copies when you're ready to plan your own second version of this quilt!

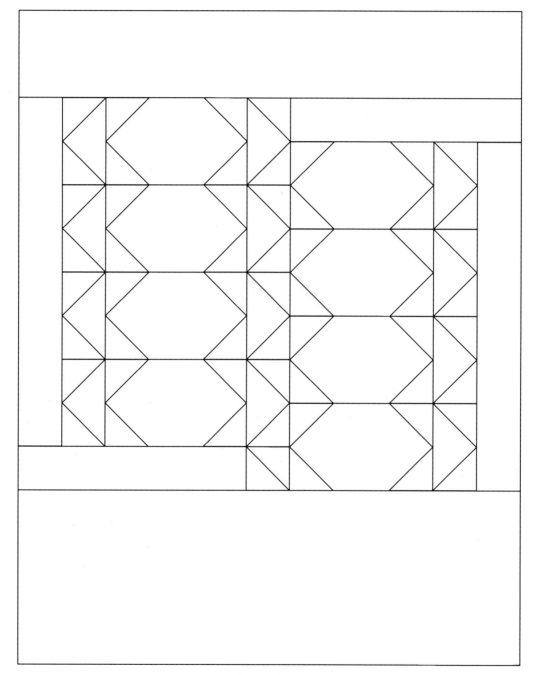

Design sheet

"Morse Code: Midnight Woods," 80½" x 88½",
designed by Deanne Moore; pieced by Terry Hughes; quilted by Guy and Kathy Ackerson.

*W*ith a symmetrical arrangement of dots and dashes, this full-size quilt can take on a clean, crisp, and modern look, a fun and whimsical style, or a pretty, traditional flavor, depending on the fabrics chosen.

Materials

Yardage is based on 42"-wide fabric.

¼ yard *each* of 16 assorted taupe prints for blocks and inner border

3 yards of dark-blue print for background

2½ yards of leaf print for outer border and binding

⅝ yard of light-blue print for strip sets and middle border

7½ yards of fabric for backing

89" x 97" piece of batting

Cutting

From the dark-blue print, cut:
18 strips, 2½" x 42"; crosscut *1 of the strips* into
    2 rectangles, 2½" x 6½"
8 strips, 6½" x 42"; crosscut into:
    4 strips, 6½" x 30½"
    4 strips, 6½" x 23½"
    4 rectangles, 6½" x 16½"
    4 rectangles, 6½" x 9½"

From the light-blue print, cut:
2 strips, 2½" x 42"
8 strips, 1½" x 42"

From *each* of the assorted taupe prints, cut:
1 strip, 6½" x 42"; crosscut into:
    1 rectangle, 6½" x 12½" (16 total)
    3 rectangles, 2½" x 6½" (48 total)

From the *lengthwise grain* of the leaf print, cut:
4 strips, 6½" x 80"
5 strips, 2¼" x 72"

Making the Strip Sets

Refer to "Strip Sets" on page 77. Sew a dark-blue 2½"-wide strip to each long edge of a light-blue 2½"-wide strip to make a strip set. Make two strip sets. From the strip sets, cut 25 segments, 2½" wide.

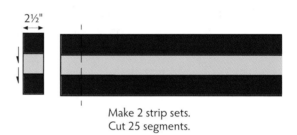

Make 2 strip sets.
Cut 25 segments.

Assembling the Quilt Top

Referring to the photo on page 65 and the assembly diagram on page 67, arrange the pieces on a design wall or other flat surface. Rearrange the taupe 6½" x 12½" rectangles until you're pleased with their placement.

1. Sew dark-blue 30½"-long strips to opposite sides of one strip-set segment to make row 1. Press the seam allowances toward the dark-blue strips. Repeat to make row 9.

2. Join two of the dark-blue 23½"-long strips, two strip-set segments, and one taupe 6½" x 12½" rectangle to make row 2. Press the seam allowances toward the rectangles. Repeat to make row 8.

3. Join two of the dark-blue 16½"-long rectangles, three strip-set segments, and two taupe rectangles to make row 3. Press the seam allowances toward the rectangles. Repeat to make row 7.

4. Join two of the dark-blue 6½" x 9½" rectangles, four strip-set segments, and three taupe rectangles to make row 4. Press the seam allowances toward the rectangles. Repeat to make row 6.

5. Join the dark-blue 2½" x 6½" rectangles, five strip-set segments, and four taupe rectangles to make row 5. Press the seam allowances toward the rectangles.

6. Join the remaining dark-blue 2½"-wide strips end to end. Measure each of the pieced rows; they should measure 62½" long. From the pieced strip, cut eight strips to this length. Join the dark-blue strips and pieced rows as shown below to complete the quilt-top center.

7. To make the pieced side border, sew 13 taupe 2½" x 6½" rectangles together end to end to make a side inner-border strip. Press the seam

allowances in one direction. Make two. To make the pieced top border, sew 11 taupe 2½" x 6½" rectangles together end to end. Press the seam allowances in one direction. Repeat to make the pieced bottom border.

Side borders.
Make 2.

Top/bottom borders.
Make 2.

8. Refer to "Borders" on page 78 to measure the length of the quilt top. Trim the pieced side borders to this length and sew them to the sides of the quilt top. Press the seam allowances toward the quilt-top center. Measure the width of the quilt top. Trim the pieced top and bottom borders to this length and sew them to the top and bottom of the quilt in the same manner.

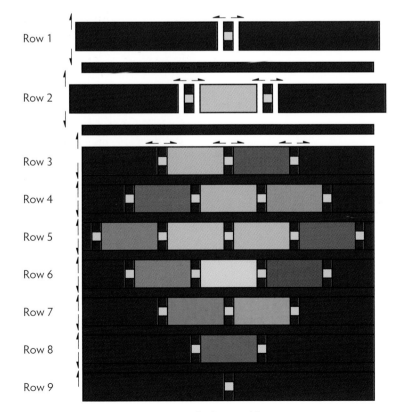

Quilt assembly

9. Join the light-blue 1½"-wide strips end to end. Measure, cut, and sew the strips to the sides, top, and bottom of the quilt for the middle border. Press all seam allowances toward the middle-border strips.

10. Join the leaf-print 6½"-wide strips end to end. Measure, cut, and sew the strips to the sides, top, and bottom of the quilt for the outer border. Press all seam allowances toward the outer-border strips.

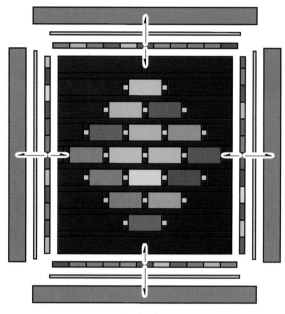

Quilt plan

Finishing

Choose a quilting design that enhances the look and style of your quilt. Layer the quilt top, backing, and batting for quilting, or deliver them to your professional long-arm machine quilter. Referring to "Binding" on page 78, use the leaf-print 2¼"-wide strips to make and attach the binding. Attach a quilt label to the back.

Change the Fabric ↻ *Change the Quilt*

Imagine this quilt made with . . .
- A rainbow of solid colors on a neutral background
- Children's prints
- Florals
- Batiks

"Morse Code: Missouri Connection," 80½" x 88½", designed by Deanne Moore; pieced by Terry Hughes; quilted by Guy and Kathy Ackerson.

It's Your Turn to Play!

Now it's your turn to play with fabrics and colors to make this project uniquely your own. You may want to make several photocopies of this design sheet. Use the sheets to experiment with different color combinations *before* you head to the quilt shop. Then you can make more copies when you're ready to plan your own second version of this quilt!

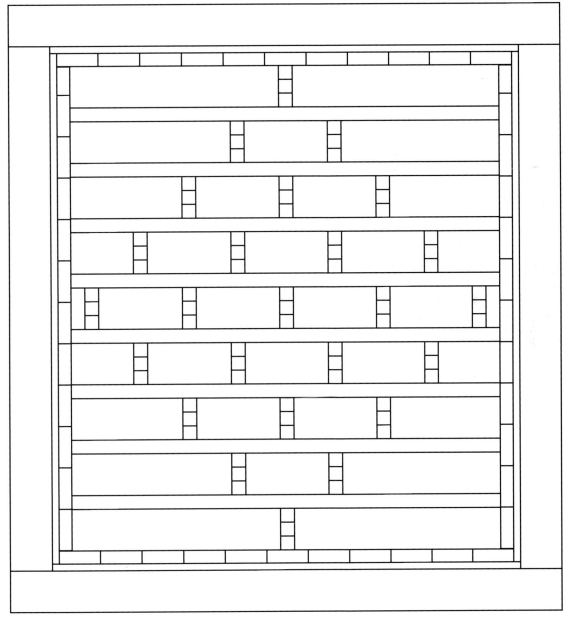

Design sheet

Pegasus

"Pegasus: Topaz," 61¾" x 73½",
designed by Deanne Moore; pieced by Maggi Oswald; quilted by Patricia Ritter.

The unusual treatment of a traditional quilt block gives rise to a structured mosaic look, and lets this quilt take wing. This design goes from mild to wild, depending on the style and color palette, and is sure to garner attention no matter what fabrics you use.

Materials

Yardage is based on 42"-wide fabric.

2¼ yards of green shot cotton for setting rectangles and binding*

2 yards of chartreuse tone on tone for blocks and setting rectangles

1¼ yards of navy tone on tone for block backgrounds

⅞ yard of multicolored print for blocks

¾ yard for green polka dot for border

⅜ yard of pink print for block centers

4 yards of fabric for backing

70" x 82" piece of batting

A shot cotton uses one color thread for the warp and a different color thread for the weft, giving the fabric depth and visual interest. If you prefer, you can substitute a solid fabric.

Cutting

From the navy tone on tone, cut:
5 strips, 4⅞" x 42"; crosscut into 33 squares, 4⅞" x 4⅞"
3 strips, 4½" x 42"; crosscut into 22 squares, 4½" x 4½"

From the multicolored print, cut:
5 strips, 4⅞" x 42"; crosscut into 33 squares, 4⅞" x 4⅞"

From the pink print, cut:
2 strips, 4½" x 42"; crosscut into 11 squares, 4½" x 4½"

From the chartreuse tone on tone, cut:
8 strips, 6½" x 42"; crosscut into 44 squares, 6½" x 6½"
2 strips, 6⅛" x 42"; crosscut into 12 squares, 6⅛" x 6⅛"

From the green shot cotton, cut:
3 strips, 11¾" x 42"; crosscut into:
    8 rectangles, 9" x 11¾"
    2 rectangles, 11¾" x 17½"
2 strips, 9" x 34¼"
8 strips, 2¼" x 42"

From the green polka dot, cut:
7 strips, 3" x 42"

Making the Blocks

1. Refer to "Half-Square-Triangle Units" on page 76. Sew a navy 4⅞" square and a multicolored 4⅞" square together to make two half-square-triangle units. Make a total of 66 units.

Make 66.

2. Sew six half-square-triangle units, one pink 4½" square, and two blue 4½" squares together as shown to make a block. The block should measure 12½" x 12½". Make a total of 11 blocks.

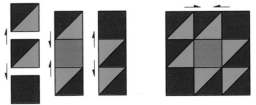

Make 11.

3. Trim the navy squares on each block as shown, making sure to leave ¼" beyond the outer points for seam allowances.

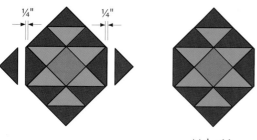

Make 11.

4. With a chartreuse 6½" square right side up, place a block wrong side up atop the square. Align the edge of the trimmed navy square with an edge of the chartreuse square and the corner of the block with the edge of the square as shown. Pin and sew ¼" from the raw edge of the block. Trim away the excess chartreuse triangle. Turn the unit over and press the seam allowances toward the triangle.

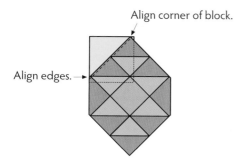

Align corner of block.

Align edges. →

5. In the same way, sew chartreuse squares to the remaining three sides of the block as shown. Trim the oversized chartreuse triangles, making sure to leave ¼" beyond all points for seam allowances. The rectangular block should measure 11¾" x 17½". Make 11.

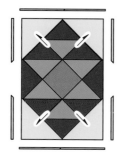

Trim.
Make 11.

Making the Setting Pieces

Refer to "Stitch-and-Flip Corners" on page 77 as needed.

1. Sew a chartreuse 6⅛" square to the upper-right corner of a green 9" x 11¾" rectangle to make unit A. Press the resulting triangle open. Make four units.

2. Sew a chartreuse 6⅛" square to the upper-left corner of a green 9" x 11¾" rectangle to make unit B. Press the resulting triangle open. Make four units.

Unit A.
Make 4.

Unit B.
Make 4.

3. Sew chartreuse 6⅛" squares to the upper-right and upper-left corners of a green 11¾" x 17½" rectangle to make unit C. Press the resulting triangles open. Make two units.

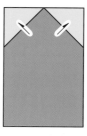

Unit C.
Make 2.

Assembling the Quilt Top

Refer to the photo on page 70 and the quilt assembly diagram on page 73 for placement guidance throughout. After sewing each seam, press the seam allowances in the directions indicated.

1. Sew C units to each end of one block, rotating one unit as shown, to make the center column.

2. Sew together two blocks, one A unit, and one B unit to make an inner column. Make two.

3. Join the inner columns to the center column. Then sew green 9" x 34¼" strips to the top and bottom of the three-column section to complete the center section.

4. Sew together three blocks, one A unit, and one B unit to make an outer column. Make two.

5. Sew the outer columns to the center section to complete the quilt-top center.

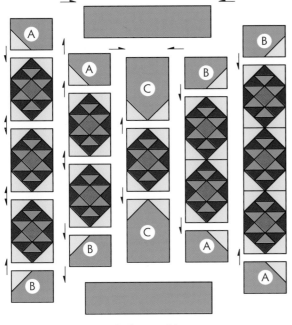

Quilt assembly

6. Join the green polka-dot strips end to end. Refer to "Borders" on page 78 to measure the length of the quilt top. From the pieced strip, cut two strips to this length and sew them to the sides of the quilt top. Press the seam allowances toward the border. Measure the width of the quilt top. From the remainder of the pieced strip, cut two strips to this length and sew them to the top and bottom of the quilt top. Press the seam allowances toward the border.

Finishing

Choose a quilting design that enhances the look and style of your quilt. Layer the quilt top, backing, and batting for quilting, or deliver them to your professional long-arm machine quilter. Referring to "Binding" on page 78, use the green strips to make and attach the binding. Attach a quilt label to the back.

Change the Fabric Change the Quilt

Imagine this quilt made with . . .
- Batiks
- Civil War reproduction prints
- Black-and-white prints
- Scraps

"Pegasus: Lampasas," 61¾" x 73½", designed by Deanne Moore; pieced and quilted by Dea Heller.

It's Your Turn to Play!

Now it's your turn to play with fabrics and colors to make this project uniquely your own. You may want to make several photocopies of this design sheet. Use the sheets to experiment with different color combinations *before* you head to the quilt shop. Then you can make more copies when you're ready to plan your own second version of this quilt!

Design sheet

Go-To Techniques

A few basic quiltmaking techniques are used repeatedly in the projects in this book. Detailed instructions are included here for making half-square-triangle units, flying-geese units (two methods), strip sets, stitch-and-flip corners, borders, and binding.

Basic Tools

I wouldn't be comfortable beginning a project without the following supplies.

Rotary-cutting tools: A self-healing cutting mat (18" x 24" or larger), a rotary cutter with a fresh blade, and an assortment of acrylic rulers. My go-to rulers are a 6" x 24", a 6" square, and a 15" square, all with 45° lines.

Pressing tools: Ironing board or pad with a non-shifting cover and minimal loft, and an iron with steam capability and a clean, nonstick surface.

Marking tools: Mechanical pencil with 0.5 mm lead (my preference) for marking light fabrics. Silver or white quilter's pencils are better for marking dark fabrics.

Sewing tools: A clean and oiled sewing machine with plenty of empty bobbins, a ¼" presser foot, and a walking foot. Good-quality, neutral-colored cotton sewing thread. A new needle for each project (I usually use a 70/10 Microtex Sharp needle). Fine, sharp glass-head pins. Small, sharp fabric scissors and, yes, a seam ripper.

Cutting Basics

Take an extra bit of time to prepare your fabric for accurate, straight-of-grain cutting. If the fabric is badly creased or wrinkled, press your fabric before cutting. Fold the fabric in half, aligning the selvage edges. Lay the fabric on the cutting mat with the folded edge toward you. Place a 6" x 24" ruler along the right edge of the fabric, with a horizontal line of the ruler aligned with the fold and the right cutting edge just inside all the layers of fabric. Starting at the fold, make a cut by

sliding the cutter away from you along the long edge of the ruler.

Rotate the mat 180°, being careful that the fabric doesn't shift. To cut a strip, place the long ruler so it overlaps the fabric and align the marking for the desired width even with the cut (left) edge of the fabric. (*Reverse if you are left-handed.*)

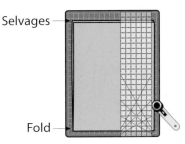

Align a horizontal mark on the ruler with the fold. Cut along the edge of the ruler.

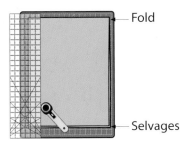

Align fabric edge with mark on the ruler.

Machine Piecing

Position pieces right sides together, and use a consistent and accurate ¼" seam allowance. If your pieces aren't fitting together accurately, the most likely culprit is your seam allowance. Check your seam allowances using the ¼" lines on an acrylic ruler. If the seam allowance is too wide or too narrow, use masking tape or a permanent pen to mark the bed of your machine, or adjust the needle position on your sewing machine. For either method, sew on a piece of graph paper with ¼" grid lines to determine the ¼" position.

Half-Square-Triangle Units

Half-square-triangle units are made in pairs, using one square each of two different fabrics. The squares are cut ⅞" larger than the desired finished size of the half-square-triangle unit. Or, you can cut the squares 1" larger, and then trim the unfinished unit to the desired size.

1. Begin with two same-sized squares from different fabrics. Draw a diagonal line from corner to corner on the wrong side of the lighter square.

2. Place the squares right sides together, with the marked square on top. Stitch ¼" from each side of the drawn line. Cut the squares apart on the drawn line.

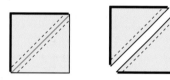

3. Press the seam allowances to one side, usually toward the darker fabric, being careful not to distort the unit. Trim off the little triangles that extend beyond the unit.

Flying-Geese Units

I use two different methods for making flying-geese units. When making multiple units (three or more) that all need the same background fabric, I use method A. This method produces four identical units at a time. Even if one or two units are extra, this method is simple and doesn't waste any fabric. When I only need one or two units, or when a pattern requires different background fabrics, I use method B.

Method A. This method uses one large square and four small squares to make four flying-geese units at one time. The finished units are rectangular and the long side measures twice the size of the short side (for example, 2" x 4"). The large square is always cut 1¼" larger than the finished size of the long side, and the small squares are always cut ⅞" larger than the finished size of the short side. For a 2" x 4" finished unit, you would cut one 5¼" square and four 2⅞" squares.

1. Draw a diagonal line from corner to corner on the wrong side of each of the four small squares.

2. With right sides together, place two small squares on opposite corners of the large square, aligning the raw edges. The points of the small squares will overlap in the center of the large square, and the drawn line should extend from corner to corner as shown.

3. Sew ¼" from each side of the drawn line. Cut the squares apart on the drawn line. Press the seam allowances toward the small triangles.

4. With right sides together, place the remaining marked squares on the corners of each piece, aligning the raw edges. The drawn line should extend from the point of the corner to the point between the two small triangles. Sew ¼" from each side of the drawn line. Cut the pieces apart on the drawn line. Press the seam allowances toward the small triangles. You'll

have four flying-geese units. Trim off the little triangles that extend beyond the units.

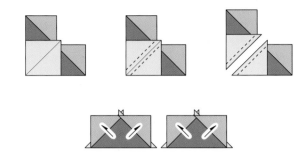

Method B. This method uses one rectangle and two squares to make one flying-geese unit. The finished unit is rectangular and the long side measures twice the size of the short side (for example, 2" x 4"). The rectangle is cut ½" larger than the finished size of the unit and the squares are cut ½" larger than the finished size of the short side. For a 2" x 4" finished unit, you would cut one 2½" x 4½" rectangle and two 2½" squares.

1. Draw a diagonal line from corner to corner on the wrong side of each square.

2. Place a marked square on one end of the rectangle, right sides together and raw edges aligned. Sew on the drawn line. Trim away the excess corner fabric, leaving a ¼" seam allowance. Press the resulting triangle open.

3. Place the other marked square on the opposite end of the rectangle, right sides together and edges aligned as shown. Sew on the drawn line, trim away the excess corner fabric, and press the resulting triangle open.

Strip Sets

Making strip sets is a fast and simple way to piece multiple units of rectangles or squares. They can be composed of any number of strips. The strips can be the same or different widths.

Refer to the project instructions to sew the strips together in the correct order, along their long edges. When adding strips, sew from the opposite end each time to help avoid distortion of your strip set. (Horizontal arrows indicate stitching directions.) Using a walking foot will also prevent distortion. Press the seam allowances as indicated.

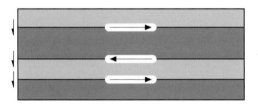

To cut segments, straighten the right end of the strip set by aligning horizontal lines on the ruler with seams on the strip set. Cut along the right edge of the ruler. Place the straightened end of the strip set on the left and align the required measurement on the ruler with the cleanly cut edge of the strip set. Cut the specified number of segments. After cutting a few segments, check that your cuts are at right angles to the seam and square up again if needed.

Stitch-and-Flip Corners

Corners can be added to any size square or rectangle using this method. You'll start with a large square or rectangle and a small square.

1. Draw a diagonal line from corner to corner on the wrong side of the small square.

2. Place the marked square on one corner of the large square or rectangle, right sides together. Sew on the drawn line. Trim the excess corner fabric, leaving a ¼" seam allowance. Press the seam allowances toward the resulting triangle.

Borders

Single or multiple borders are added to frame a single block, piece of fabric, or an entire quilt top. The conventional order is to sew border strips to the long sides of the center unit first, and then sew them to the top and bottom.

Borders made from a single fabric are pieced end to end, if necessary, and then trimmed to the exact length required before sewing. Otherwise the borders may be too long, and result in wavy or rippling edges. Sometimes it's more efficient to cut strips from the lengthwise grain of the fabric, instead of piecing many strips together. Since seam allowances vary from one quilter to another, you should cut your borders to fit the measurements of your actual quilt top.

1. Measure the length of the quilt top from top to bottom through the center and along each side. If the measurements differ, calculate the average by adding the three measurements together and then dividing by three. Cut two border strips to the length determined, piecing as necessary. Pin-mark the center of the border strips and the sides of the quilt top.

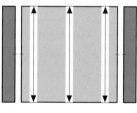

Measure in three places
top to bottom.

2. Pin the borders to the sides of the quilt top, matching centers and ends. Sew the side border strips in place with a ¼" seam allowance. Press the seam allowances toward the border strips.

3. Measure the width of the quilt top from side to side through the center and each end (including the side borders just added) and determine the average. Cut two strips to this

measurement, piecing as necessary. Pin and sew the top and bottom borders in place; press.

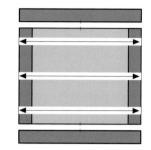

Measure in three places
side to side.

Quilting Designs

The actual quilting makes a great impact on the look of your finished quilt. Hand quilting versus machine quilting, custom versus edge-to-edge quilting, light versus heavy, and choice of thread color(s) and batting loft offer endless options. Choose a quilting style and pattern that complements the quilt, in whatever way feels right to *you*. Visit your local quilt shop for ideas, study the quilting on quilts displayed at quilt shows and museums, and look at the quilting on the projects shown in books. It's so easy to get caught up in the fabrics and colors used in the quilt construction that the actual quilting is often overlooked! If you use a professional quilter, ask for ideas and suggestions, just as you may have when you chose the fabrics, but *make the choice yourself*—it's *your* quilt!

Binding

The quilts in this book all have double-fold binding. Since you'll be sewing through many layers, I recommend using a walking foot to attach the binding to your quilt.

1. Join the strips at right angles, right sides together, and stitch diagonally across the corner as shown. Trim the excess fabric, leaving ¼" for seam allowances. Press the seam allowances open to distribute bulk. Press the

strip in half lengthwise, wrong sides together and raw edges aligned.

2. Trim the batting and backing so the edges are even with the quilt top.

3. Start the binding in the middle of one side of your quilt front, aligning the raw edges of the binding with the raw edges of the quilt. Pin the binding end in place. Loosely run the binding around the perimeter of the quilt, checking to see if a binding seam falls within 2" to 3" of a corner. (It's difficult to achieve nice-looking mitered corners if there are additional layers of fabric from a seam allowance on a corner!) If a seam is near a corner, move the starting point of the binding and recheck the position around the quilt.

4. Begin stitching 10" to 12" from the pinned end of the binding strip with a backstitch. Using a ¼" seam allowance, sew to exactly ¼" from the first corner and backstitch.

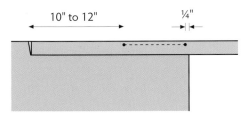

5. Remove the quilt from the machine. Fold the binding up, away from the next side of the quilt, so that the fold creates a 45° angle. Bring the binding back down onto itself, even with the raw edge of the quilt top. Beginning at the fold, backstitch, stitch along the edge of the quilt top, and stop ¼" from the next corner. Repeat for all sides of the quilt

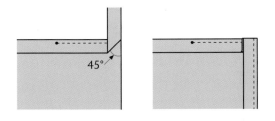

6. Stop stitching 12" to 15" from the pinned starting end of the binding strip with a backstitch. Lay the binding strip along the edge of the quilt and trim off any excess length so that the ending tail is about 1" from the beginning backstitch. Unfold the binding tail and lay it flat on the quilt top, right side facing up.

7. Unfold the beginning tail of the binding strip, then fold the end under at a 45° angle, wrong sides together. Finger-press the fold. Place the beginning tail atop the ending tail as shown.

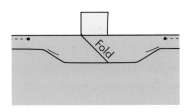

8. Hold the two ends together and unfold the top strip so that the strips are at right angles, right sides together. Pin the strips together, with the pins parallel to the fold. Sew on the fold line, remove the pins, and check that the binding fits the unstitched space. Then trim the excess fabric, leaving a ¼" seam allowance. Press the seam allowances open.

Unstitched quilt edge

9. Refold the binding, position it along the quilt, and finish stitching it in place.

10. Fold the binding over the raw edges of the quilt, with the folded edge covering the row of machine stitching. Hand or machine stitch the binding to the quilt, folding the miters as you reach each corner. Stitch the miters in place.

About the Author

Deanne Moore lives with her four children in central Texas, where she has owned a quilt shop since 2002. She enjoys teaching and has taught classes on a wide variety of quiltmaking techniques and projects in her shop and for guilds in the region for over 10 years. She frequently gives presentations and lectures to guilds, quilt shops, and groups of shop owners. In 2005, she began designing quilt patterns for use in her shop, and is now constantly delighted when her customers report seeing her published patterns in quilt shops all over the country, and on blogs and websites too. Her quilt patterns have been published in national and international magazines, and she works closely with many major fabric companies on cross-promotional campaigns.

In her former life, Deanne did biochemical research, plus she taught college chemistry for many years and high-school math and science for a few. In her free time, she enjoys the company and activities of her children, and the freedom of the open road. Escaping for a scenic drive on an unexplored country road is a favorite pastime. Since starting to design quilting patterns, she has found that any place can be a happy place when she has a graph-paper notebook in hand. After all, ideas and inspiration occur at the most unexpected times and places.

Acknowledgments

The quilts shown in this book were pieced, quilted, and finished by a team of the most enthusiastic, generous, and adventurous quilters I know: Kathy and Guy Ackerson, Caroline Dunda, Shirley Ginn, Mary Jane Heinen, Dea Heller, Terry Hughes, Wendy Kinard, Nita Leinneweber, Maggi Oswald, Patricia Ritter, Laurie Shook, Kelleigh Sommer, and Diane Tarpey. They have my eternal gratitude!

My daughter Tori Quill helped me tremendously with editing and changes in the early stages of the manuscript, and Kelleigh Sommer did what she does best—kept me (relatively) sane and organized while devoting her attention to so many of the small details. Heartfelt thanks to them both.